casseroles

casseroles

over 160 step-by-step recipes

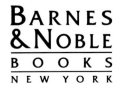

BARNES
&NOBLE
BOOKS
NEW YORK

This edition published by Barnes & Noble, Inc.,
by arrangement with Salamander Books Ltd.

2003 Barnes and Noble Books

ISBN 0-7607-3359-7

© Salamander Books Ltd 2003

A member of **Chrysalis** Books plc

A CIP catalog record for this book is available from the
Library of Congress.

CREDITS
Project managed by Stella Caldwell
Editor: Anne McDowall
Filmset by SX Composing DTP, England
Printed in China

CONTENTS

INTRODUCTION

Chicken or meat, vegetables and stock cooked slowly in the oven or on top of the stove – the ultimate in comfort food, or a special dish for a dinner party. This is cooking at its most simple – everything goes in one pot – and at its most delicious – food cooked in this way retains all its flavor and succulence.

Many of these recipes are classics from around the world, from the French Coq au Vin and Boeuf en Daube Provençal to the North African Tagine, east to India and Malaysia for spice-filled curries, and on to the Caribbean for Chicken Pelau and Jamaican Pepperpot. The recipes in *Casseroles* include not only meat or poultry dishes that are braised slowly in the oven, but also others that are cooked in one pot in liquid, either on the stove or in the oven. There are also many vegetarian and fish dishes.

In many of these recipes the meat and vegetables are browned or softened first on top of the stove before being cooked slowly and gently. Browning meat is not essential, but it does deepen the color of the sauce, while vegetables take on a sweeter flavor if they are sautéed in a little oil or butter first. Long gentle cooking gives the meat a special tenderness and brings out its flavor to the full, while the vegetables and other ingredients add their goodness to the juices. Marinating is also sometimes used in the recipes. Again, this is not essential, but it does add moisture to lean meat, which can be rather dry, and it is also good for tenderizing tougher cuts of meat.

Investing in good-quality cookware is well worthwhile. When buying cookware it is important to be aware of the difference between flameproof and ovenproof items as some pieces of equipment can only be used with one source of heat. Ideally, choose cookware that is suitable for using both on the hob and in the oven. (This is more economical too, as you only need to buy one piece of equipment instead of two.) Always buy the best you can afford: better materials give better cooking results and will last much longer than cheaper versions.

VEGETABLES
& VEGETARIAN

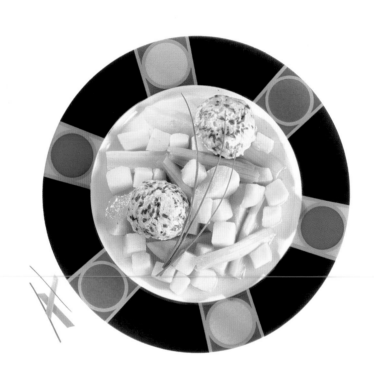

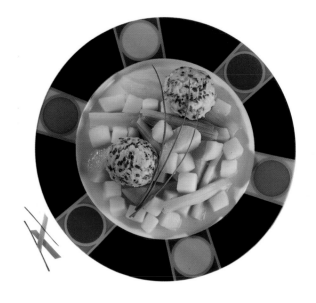

RATATOUILLE

2 eggplants, sliced
3 zucchini, sliced
3 or 4 tablespoons olive oil
1 Spanish onion, very thinly sliced
3 cloves garlic, crushed
2 large red bell peppers, thinly sliced
4 ripe beefsteak tomatoes, peeled, seeded, and
   chopped
few sprigs thyme, marjoram and oregano
salt and freshly ground black pepper
2 tablespoons chopped fresh parsley
2 tablespoons chopped fresh basil

Put eggplant and zucchini in a colander, sprinkle with salt and leave 1 hour.

Rinse well, drain, and dry thoroughly with absorbent kitchen paper. Heat 2 tablespoons oil in a heavy flameproof casserole, add eggplant, and cook, stirring occasionally, a few minutes. Add 1 tablespoon oil, onion, and garlic and cook, stirring occasionally, 2 to 3 minutes. Add peppers and cook, stirring occasionally, 1 to 2 minutes.

Add zucchini to casserole with more oil if necessary. Cook, stirring occasionally, 2 to 3 minutes, then add tomatoes and thyme, marjoram, and oregano leaves. Season lightly with salt and pepper, cover, and cook very gently 30 to 40 minutes, stirring occasionally. Stir in parsley and basil and cook, uncovered, 5 to 10 minutes, until liquid has evaporated. Serve warm or cold.

Makes 4 servings.

LEEK STEW WITH DUMPLINGS

1½ lb. leeks, halved lengthwise
2 medium potatoes, diced
8 oz. Jerusalem artichokes, peeled and quartered
4 cups vegetable stock
salt
fresh chives, to garnish
DUMPLINGS:
1 cup self-rising flour
½ cup vegetable suet
2-3 cups chopped fresh chives

Cut leeks into 3 in. lengths. Put leeks, potatoes and artichokes in a large flameproof casserole.

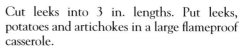

Add stock and season with salt. Bring to a boil, cover, and simmer 45 to 60 minutes. Meanwhile, to make dumplings, put flour, suet, and chives in a large bowl, season with salt, and mix well. Stir in ¼ cup water and bind to a dough. Knead lightly and let rest 5 minutes.

Shape dough into eight small dumplings. Place dumplings around the outside of the vegetable mixture. Cover and simmer 30 minutes. Garnish with chives and serve.

Makes 4 servings.

BRAISED FENNEL PROVENÇAL

3 fennel bulbs, trimmed
3 tablespoons olive oil
4 cloves garlic, peeled
1 lb. ripe plum tomatoes, peeled, seeded, and diced
   (see page 12)
⅔ cup dry white wine
12 Niçoise olives
4 sprigs thyme
2 bay leaves
pinch sugar
salt and pepper
thyme sprigs, to garnish

Cut fennel bulbs lengthwise into ½ in. slices.

Heat oil in a large skillet and fry fennel slices and garlic 4 to 5 minutes on each side until golden; remove from pan with a slotted spoon and reserve.

Add tomatoes and wine to the pan and boil rapidly 5 minutes. Stir in olives, thyme, bay leaves, and sugar and arrange fennel slices over the top, in a single layer if possible. Cover and simmer gently 20 minutes, season, and serve hot. Alternatively, let cool and serve at room temperature, garnished with thyme.

Makes 4 servings.

MUSHROOM RATATOUILLE

¼ cup dried porcini (mushrooms)
14½ oz. can chopped tomatoes
3 tablespoons olive oil
1 clove garlic, crushed
1 tablespoon chopped fresh basil
1 large onion, chopped
2 teaspoons chopped fresh thyme
1 lb 2 oz. mixed mushrooms, wiped
salt and pepper
French bread, to serve

Place porcini in a small bowl and pour over ⅔ cup boiling water. Set aside 20 minutes to soak. Strain, reserving liquid, chop porcini, and reserve.

Place tomatoes, 1 tablespoon of oil, garlic, and basil in a pan. Bring to a boil and simmer 20 minutes.

Meanwhile, heat remaining oil in a large skillet and fry onion and thyme 5 minutes. Add porcini and fresh mushrooms and stir-fry over a high heat 3 to 4 minutes until golden. Add porcini liquid and simmer 3 minutes, stir in tomato sauce, and simmer gently an additional 5 minutes. Season and serve hot, warm, or cold with crisp French bread.

Makes 4 to 6 servings.

BELL PEPPER & EGGPLANT

2 eggplants, cut into large cubes
2 red bell peppers, diced
2 yellow bell peppers, diced
2 cloves garlic, crushed
1 bunch scallions, cut into ½ in. lengths
¾ cup tomato juice
1 cup canned chopped tomatoes
2 tablespoons chopped fresh mixed herbs
few drops Tabasco sauce
salt and freshly ground black pepper
oregano leaves, to garnish

Preheat oven to 350F. Place eggplant cubes on a plate and sprinkle liberally with salt. Let stand 30 minutes.

Rinse eggplant, drain thoroughly, and pat dry with absorbent kitchen paper. Place eggplant, bell peppers, garlic, and scallions in an ovenproof casserole and mix well. Add tomato juice, chopped tomatoes, herbs, Tabasco sauce, and salt and pepper and stir to combine.

Cover and cook in the oven 45 minutes, stirring occasionally. Garnish with oregano leaves and serve with freshly cooked pasta.

Makes 6 servings.

VEGETABLE COUSCOUS

3 tablespoons olive oil
1 onion, chopped
2 cloves garlic, crushed
1 teaspoon ground cumin
1 teaspoon paprika
1¼ cups vegetable stock
14½ oz. can tomatoes
1 cinnamon stick
pinch saffron threads
4 baby eggplants, quartered
8 baby zucchini, trimmed
8 baby carrots
salt
15 oz. can chickpeas, drained
1 cup ready-to-eat prunes
1¼ cups couscous
3 tablespoons chopped fresh parsley
3 tablespoons chopped cilantro
2 or 3 tablespoons harissa

Heat olive oil in a large saucepan. Add onion and garlic and cook gently 5 minutes until soft. Add cumin and paprika and cook, stirring, 1 minute. Add stock, tomatoes, cinnamon, saffron, eggplants, zucchini, and carrots. Season with salt. Bring to a boil, cover, and cook 20 minutes until vegetables are just tender.

Add chickpeas and prunes and cook 10 minutes. Meanwhile, put couscous in a bowl and cover generously with boiling water. Leave 10 minutes, then drain thoroughly and fluff up with a fork. Stir parsley and cilantro into vegetables. Heap couscous onto a warmed serving plate. Remove vegetables with a slotted spoon and arrange on top. Spoon over a little sauce. Stir harissa into remaining sauce and serve separately.

Makes 4 servings.

LENTIL & BEAN CHILI

1 tablespoon olive oil
1 onion, chopped
1 clove garlic, chopped
¾ cup green lentils
1¼ cups vegetable stock
1 teaspoon mild chili powder
14½ oz. can chopped tomatoes
1 green bell pepper, chopped
15 oz. can red kidney beans in chili sauce
salt and freshly ground black pepper
chopped fresh Italian parsley, to garnish

Heat oil in a flameproof casserole and cook onion and garlic until soft. Add lentils, stock, chili powder, and tomatoes.

Cover and simmer gently 30 to 40 minutes, until lentils are almost cooked.

Stir in green bell pepper and kidney beans and their sauce and simmer 10 to 15 minutes, until lentils are cooked and liquid has been absorbed. Season with salt and pepper. Garnish with chopped parsley and serve.

Makes 4 servings.

MOROCCAN CASSEROLE

2 tablespoons olive oil
1 large onion, chopped
1 large eggplant, cut into chunks
2 cloves garlic, crushed
1 teaspoon ground cumin
1 teaspoon turmeric
1 teaspoon ground ginger
1 teaspoon paprika
1 teaspoon ground allspice
3 × 14½ oz. cans chopped tomatoes
15 oz. can chickpeas, drained
½ cup raisins
1 tablespoon chopped cilantro
3 tablespoons chopped fresh parsley
salt and freshly ground black pepper

Heat oil in a flameproof casserole. Add onion and cook, stirring occasionally, 5 minutes, until soft. Add eggplant, cover and cook 5 minutes. Add garlic, ground cumin, turmeric, ground ginger, paprika, and allspice and cook, stirring, 1 minute.

Stir in tomatoes, chickpeas, raisins, and chopped cilantro and parsley. Season with salt and pepper. Bring to a boil and simmer 45 minutes. Serve.

Makes 4 to 6 servings.

BROCCOLI WITH CHILI DRESSING

2 lb. ripe tomatoes
3 tablespoons olive oil
1 clove garlic, crushed
2 teaspoons lemon juice
1 teaspoon hot chili sauce
1 teaspoon balsamic vinegar
1 medium bunch broccoli
¼ cup pitted black olives, sliced
¼ cup pine nuts, toasted
1 tablespoon chopped fresh parsley
¼ cup Parmesan shavings

Place tomatoes in a large heatproof bowl and pour over boiling water to cover.

Leave 1 minute, then drain, refresh under cold water, and pat dry. Peel, discard skins and seeds, and finely chop flesh. Heat oil in a large saucepan, add tomatoes, garlic, lemon juice, chili sauce, and vinegar. Bring to a boil, cover, and cook 10 minutes. Uncover, increase heat, and cook until slightly reduced and thickened.

Meanwhile, trim broccoli and steam 5 minutes. Add to sauce with olives, pine nuts, and parsley and stir well until combined. Transfer to a warmed serving dish, sprinkle over Parmesan shavings, and serve at once.

Makes 4 servings.

Note: For vegans, omit Parmesan cheese.

BROCCOLI CAPONATA

2 tablespoons olive oil
1 red onion, chopped
1 red bell pepper, seeded and chopped
1 clove garlic, chopped
1 teaspoon chopped fresh thyme
⅓ cup red wine
1 lb. tomatoes, peeled, seeded, and chopped (see opposite)
⅔ cup vegetable stock
1 tablespoon red wine vinegar
1 tablespoon brown sugar
1 medium bunch broccoli, trimmed and chopped
2 tablespoons tomato paste
½ cup pitted green olives
¼ cup capers, drained
1 tablespoon shredded fresh basil

In a large pan, heat oil and fry onion, bell pepper, garlic, and thyme 6 to 8 minutes until lightly browned. Add wine and boil rapidly 3 minutes. Add tomatoes, stock, vinegar, and sugar. Stir well, then cover and simmer gently 20 minutes.

Steam broccoli 5 minutes until almost cooked, add to tomato mixture with tomato paste, olives, capers, and basil. Cook an additional 3 to 4 minutes, remove from heat, and let cool. Serve at room temperature.

Makes 4 servings.

VEGETABLE & FRUIT CURRY

SAUCY BEANS

1½ teaspoons each coriander and cumin seeds
¼ cup vegetable oil
1 large onion, chopped
2 carrots, chopped
2 potatoes, diced
3 cloves garlic, crushed, or 1 tablespoon garlic purée
2 teaspoons grated fresh ginger
1 teaspoon each curry powder and turmeric
1 lb. ripe tomatoes
2 cups vegetable stock
¾ cup frozen peas, thawed
1 apple, cored and chopped
1 mango, peeled, pitted and chopped
⅔ cup cashews, toasted
1 oz. creamed coconut
1 tablespoon chopped cilantro

1 cup dried lima or pinto beans, soaked overnight in
   cold water to cover
1 bay leaf
¼ cup virgin olive oil
1 red onion, chopped
2 cloves garlic, chopped
1 tablespoon chopped fresh sage
1 lb. ripe tomatoes
1 teaspoon balsamic vinegar
salt and pepper
1 tablespoon chopped fresh parsley

Drain beans. Place in a pan with bay leaf and fresh water to cover. Bring to a boil, then simmer, covered, 40 to 45 minutes.

In a small pan, roast coriander and cumin seeds until browned and grind in a blender or spice grinder. Heat half the oil in a large pan and fry onion, carrots, and potatoes 10 minutes until browned. Heat remaining oil in a small pan and fry garlic, ginger, ground coriander and cumin seeds, curry powder, and turmeric 5 minutes. Peel, seed, and chop tomatoes (see page 12) and stir into spice mixture. Cover and cook 10 minutes. Stir into vegetable mixture with stock and simmer gently 20 minutes.

In a large pan, heat oil and fry onion, garlic, and sage 10 minutes until golden. Skin and peel tomatoes (see page 12), chop flesh, and add to the pan with vinegar. Cover and cook 5 minutes until softened.

Add peas, apple, and mango and cook an additional 5 minutes. Grind half the cashews and mix with creamed coconut. Stir in enough pan juices to form a paste and carefully stir into curry until evenly combined. Heat through and serve at once, sprinkled with whole cashews and cilantro.

Makes 4 to 6 servings.

Drain cooked beans, rinse well, and shake off excess water. Stir into onion mixture in pan, cover, and cook 4 to 5 minutes until heated through. Season to taste and sprinkle over chopped parsley. Serve with extra olive oil drizzled over beans.

Makes 4 servings.

Note: This dish is delicious served warm or cold. Pass round plenty of crusty bread to mop up juices.

MIXED VEGETABLE CURRY

CARIBBEAN RATATOUILLE

3 tablespoons vegetable oil
1 onion, sliced
1 teaspoon ground cumin
1 teaspoon chili powder
2 teaspoons ground coriander
1 teaspoon turmeric
1 large potato, diced
1 cup cauliflower florets
4 oz. green beans, sliced
2 medium carrots, diced
4 tomatoes, peeled (see page 12) and chopped
1¼ cups hot vegetable stock
onion rings, to garnish

2 tablespoons oil
1 large onion, thinly sliced
2 cloves garlic, crushed
1 red chili, seeded and finely chopped
1 eggplant, peeled and cut into 1 in. cubes
1 red bell pepper, diced
1 green bell pepper, diced
4 oz. okra, sliced
1 chayote, peeled, seeded, and chopped
1 lb. tomatoes, peeled (see page 12) and roughly chopped
1 teaspoon sugar
1 teaspoon dried thyme
2 teaspoons chopped fresh basil
salt and freshly ground black pepper
fresh basil leaves, to garnish

Heat oil in a large saucepan, add onion and fry 5 minutes, until softened. Stir in cumin, chili powder, coriander, and turmeric and cook 2 minutes, stirring occasionally. Add potatoes, cauliflower, green beans, and carrots, tossing them in spices until coated.

Heat oil in a flameproof casserole. Add onion and cook 10 minutes until soft. Stir in garlic and chili and cook an additional 2 minutes. Stir in eggplant, red and green peppers, okra, chayote, tomatoes, sugar, thyme, basil, and seasoning.

Add tomatoes and stock and cover. Bring to a boil, then reduce heat and simmer 10 to 12 minutes or until vegetables are just tender. Serve hot, garnished with onion rings.

Makes 4 servings.

Variation: Use any mixture of vegetables to make a total of 1½ lb. – turnips, rutabagas, zucchini, eggplants, parsnips and leeks are all suitable for this curry.

Cover and cook gently 20 to 30 minutes, stirring occasionally, until vegetables are almost cooked. Remove lid and simmer a few minutes until vegetables are tender and most of the liquid has evaporated. Serve hot or cold, garnished with basil leaves.

Makes 6 servings.

Variation: Vegetables may be varied according to taste and what is available. Zucchini and celery may be used instead of chayote and okra, for example.

TAMIL NADU VEGETABLES

⅔ cup red split lentils
½ teaspoon turmeric
1 small eggplant
¼ cup vegetable oil
⅓ cup dried coconut
1 teaspoon cumin seeds
½ teaspoon mustard seeds
2 dried red chilies, crushed
1 red bell pepper, seeded and sliced
1 medium zucchini, thickly sliced
3 oz. green beans, sliced
⅔ cup vegetable stock
salt
red bell pepper strips, to garnish

Wash lentils and put in a large saucepan with turmeric and 2½ cups water. Bring to a boil, then reduce heat and simmer, covered, 15 to 20 minutes, until lentils are soft. Meanwhile, cut eggplant into ½ in. dice. Heat oil in a large shallow pan, add coconut, cumin and mustard seeds, and chilies.

Fry 1 minute, then add eggplant, red bell pepper, zucchini, green beans, stock, and salt. Bring to a boil, then simmer, covered, 10 to 15 minutes, until vegetables are just tender. Stir in lentils and any cooking liquid and cook an additional 5 minutes. Serve hot, garnished with red bell pepper strips.

Makes 4 servings.

VEGETABLE & COCONUT CURRY

1 butternut squash, peeled, seeded, and diced
2 sweet potatoes, diced
2 carrots, diced
3 tablespoons oil
3 cloves garlic, crushed
1 large onion, chopped
1 fresh red chili, seeded and finely chopped
1 teaspoon ground cumin
2 teaspoons medium curry powder
2 teaspoons molasses
2 tablespoons tomato paste
2 oz. creamed coconut
salt
⅔ cup vegetable stock
finely grated zest and juice 1 lime
1 tablespoon chopped cilantro

Place squash, sweet potatoes, and carrots in a pan of salted water. Bring to a boil and simmer 5 to 8 minutes until barely tender. Drain and set aside. In a flameproof casserole heat oil. Add garlic and onion and cook 10 minutes until soft. Stir in chili, cumin, and curry powder and cook an additional minute.

Add molasses, tomato purée, and creamed coconut and cook 1 minute. Add salt, stock, lime zest and juice, and vegetables. Bring to a boil then reduce the heat, cover, and simmer gently, stirring occasionally, 10 to 15 minutes until vegetables are soft. Stir in cilantro. Serve with rice.

Makes 4 servings.

BELL PEPPER CHILI

2 onions
5 large fresh red chilies, cored, seeded, and chopped
1 red bell pepper, chopped
1 large clove garlic, chopped
2 tablespoons dry white wine
1 tablespoon olive oil
1 green bell pepper, thinly sliced
1 tablespoon tomato paste
1 teaspoon ground cumin
1 cup canned red kidney beans, drained
basil sprigs, to garnish

Roughly chop one of the onions. Put in a food processor with chilies, red bell pepper, garlic, wine, and salt. Process 2 minutes.

Slice remaining onion. Heat oil in a flameproof casserole, add sliced onion and cook, stirring occasionally, 5 minutes, until soft. Add puréed mixture, 2 tablespoons water, and green bell pepper. Bring to a boil, cover, and simmer gently 30 minutes.

Add tomato paste, cumin, and kidney beans. Simmer 10 to 15 minutes. Garnish with basil and serve.

Makes 2 to 4 servings.

MUSHROOM & BEAN CHILI

¼ cup olive oil
1 large eggplant, diced
6 oz. button mushrooms, wiped
1 large onion, chopped
1 clove garlic, chopped
1½ teaspoons paprika
½ to 1 teaspoon chili powder
1 teaspoon ground coriander
½ teaspoon ground cumin
2 lb. tomatoes, peeled and chopped
⅔ cup vegetable stock
1 oz. tortilla chips
1 tablespoon tomato paste
14½ oz. can red kidney beans
1 tablespoon chopped cilantro
salt and pepper

In a large pan, heat 2 tablespoons oil and stir-fry eggplant 10 minutes until golden, then remove from the pan with a slotted spoon and set aside. Add 1 tablespoon oil to the pan and stir-fry mushrooms until golden; remove with a slotted spoon and set aside. Add remaining oil to the pan and fry onion, garlic, paprika, ground coriander, and cumin 5 minutes. Add tomatoes and stock and cook, covered, 45 minutes.

Finely crush tortilla chips and blend with ¼ cup water and tomato paste. Whisk into chili sauce and add reserved mushrooms and eggplant. Drain beans and add to the pan with chopped cilantro. Cover and cook an additional 20 minutes. Season to taste and serve with plain boiled rice and thick sour cream, if desired.

Makes 6 servings.

Note: For vegetarians, check packet to ensure that tortilla chips are a vegetarian product.

FISH & SEAFOOD

SEAFOOD RISOTTO

1 tablespoon olive oil
6 scallions, chopped
1 clove garlic, crushed
1¼ cups risotto rice
½ teaspoon turmeric
¼ cup dry white wine
4 tomatoes, chopped
2¼ cups fish stock
1 lb. mixed cooked seafood
12 tiger shrimp
1¼ cups frozen peas
salt and freshly ground black pepper
¼ cup chopped fresh parsley

Heat oil in a large flameproof casserole. Add scallions and garlic and cook, stirring, 3 minutes, until soft. Cover and cook over a gentle heat 2 minutes. Add rice and turmeric and cook, stirring, 1 minute. Add wine, tomatoes, and half the stock to the casserole. Bring to a boil, cover and simmer 10 minutes.

Add remaining stock, bring back to a boil, cover, and cook 15 minutes, until rice has absorbed most of the liquid. Stir in seafood, shrimp, and peas, and season with salt and pepper. Cook gently, stirring occasionally, 10 minutes. Stir in parsley and serve.

Makes 4 servings.

MACKEREL WITH SOUR CREAM

4 × 4 oz. mackerel fillets, skinned
1 leek, thinly sliced
1 cup canned chopped tomatoes
1 tablespoon chopped fresh dill
½ teaspoon mild paprika
juice ½ lemon
salt
⅔ cup thick sour cream
dill sprigs, to garnish

Preheat oven to 400F. Place mackerel fillets in a shallow ovenproof dish.

In a large bowl, mix together leek, tomatoes, dill, paprika, and lemon juice and pour over mackerel. Season with salt.

Cover with a lid or piece of aluminum foil and cook in the oven 50 minutes, until fish is cooked through. Drizzle over sour cream, garnish with dill sprigs, and serve.

Makes 4 servings.

BAKED SADDLE OF SALMON

½ stick butter, softened
1 clove garlic, crushed
juice ½ lemon
2 tablespoons chopped fresh parsley
1½ lb. saddle of salmon, filleted
1 tablespoon olive oil, plus extra for greasing
6 shallots, chopped
⅔ cup fish stock
¾ cup red wine
1 cup veal stock
salt and freshly ground black pepper

In a small bowl, mix butter with garlic, lemon juice, and 1 tablespoon of chopped parsley.

Spread one of the halves of salmon with butter mixture and sandwich pieces back together. Wrap tightly in plastic wrap and put in the freezer about 1 hour to set. Do not freeze. Preheat oven to 400F. Lightly oil a large piece of aluminum foil. Take salmon out of plastic wrap and wrap tightly in aluminum foil. Place in a shallow ovenproof dish and cook in the oven 30 to 35 minutes. Remove from the dish and keep warm.

Heat oil in the dish, add shallots, and cook gently, stirring, 3 minutes, until soft. Add fish stock and red wine and boil until reduced and syrupy. Add veal stock and boil to reduce slightly. Add remaining parsley and season with salt and pepper. Divide sauce among warmed serving plates. Slice salmon, place on top of sauce, and serve.

Makes 4 servings.

TROUT WITH VEGETABLES

2 x 14½ oz. cans chopped tomatoes
1 leek, finely sliced
12 basil leaves, torn
2 teaspoons chopped fresh oregano
3 stalks celery, diced
2 zucchini, diced
¾ cup red wine
2 tablespoons red wine vinegar
4 trout, cleaned
4 basil sprigs
8 oregano sprigs

Put tomatoes, leek, torn basil, chopped oregano, celery, zucchini, wine, and vinegar in a shallow flameproof dish.

Bring to a boil, cover with a lid or piece of aluminum foil, and simmer 10 minutes. Season with salt and pepper. Stuff trout cavities with basil sprigs and half the oregano sprigs.

Place trout on top of vegetable mixture. Cover again and simmer gently 20 to 25 minutes, until trout is cooked through. Garnish with remaining oregano sprigs and serve.

Makes 4 servings.

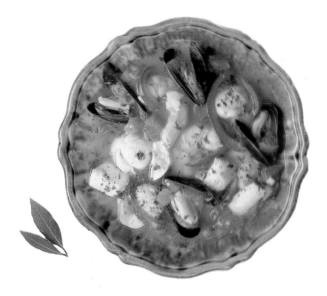

CIOPPINO

2 tablespoons light olive oil
1 large onion, chopped
3 cloves garlic, chopped
1 small red chili, seeded and thinly sliced
1 red bell pepper, seeded and sliced
1¼ lb. tomatoes
2 cups fish stock
½ cup dry white wine
1 teaspoon dried oregano
1½ teaspoons each chopped fresh thyme and marjoram
1 bay leaf
8 oz. haddock, cod, or halibut fillet, skinned
8 oz. large raw shrimp
16 mussels, cleaned
4 large scallops, shelled
2½ tablespoons chopped fresh parsley

In a large, heavy-bottomed saucepan, heat oil, add onion, garlic, chili, and red bell pepper and cook gently until onion begins to color. Meanwhile, peel, seed, and chop tomatoes (see page 12) and add to pan with stock, wine, oregano, thyme, marjoram, and bay leaf. Cover and simmer 45 minutes.

Dice fish and peel shrimp. Add mussels to pan, simmer 1 minute, then add haddock, shrimp, and scallops. Cook over a low heat 3 to 5 minutes until mussels have opened; discard any that remain closed. Sprinkle with parsley and serve at once.

Makes 4 servings.

Note: Garnish with 8 unpeeled, cooked large shrimp, if desired.

TUNA PEPERONATA

6 slices tuna, each about 1 in. thick
4 cloves garlic
⅓ cup olive oil
1 large onion, finely chopped
1 large red bell pepper, seeded, cored and thinly sliced
1 green bell pepper, seeded, cored and thinly sliced
14 oz. tomatoes, peeled (see page 12), seeded and diced
1 tablespoon sun-dried tomato paste
3 sprigs thyme
1 bay leaf
salt and pepper
parsley sprigs, to garnish

Cut slits in tuna. Cut 2 cloves of garlic into slivers and insert in slits in tuna. In a large skillet, heat half the oil, add tuna and cook until lightly browned on both sides. Remove tuna from pan and set aside. Add remaining oil to pan, add onion and bell peppers, and cook over moderate heat, stirring frequently, about 10 minutes until soft.

Chop remaining garlic, add to pan, cook 1 minute, then add tomatoes, sun-dried tomato paste, thyme, and bay leaf. Simmer, uncovered, 15 to 20 minutes, stirring occasionally. Return tuna to pan, season with salt and pepper, then cover with buttered waxed paper and cook gently 15 minutes. Serve garnished with sprigs of parsley.

Makes 6 servings.

MIXED FISH STEW

1 red mullet, red snapper, bream, or trout, weighing
    about 12 oz.
6 oz. piece sea bass
12 oz. monkfish fillet
½ bay leaf
1½ tablespoons olive oil
1 small fennel bulb
3 small carrots
1 medium onion, thinly sliced
1 small clove garlic, finely crushed
pinch saffron threads, toasted and crushed
⅔ cup dry white wine
5 tablespoons light cream
salt and pepper
½ bunch scallions, cut diagonally into thin strips
dill sprigs, to garnish

In a flameproof casserole, heat oil. Cut
fennel and carrots into thin strips and add to
casserole with onion, garlic, and saffron.
Cook 3 to 4 minutes. Add ¼ cup wine and
boil until most of the liquid has evaporated.
Add remaining wine and boil until reduced
by half.

Thickly slice mullet, snapper, bream, or trout
and place head and tail in a small saucepan.
Remove skin and bones from bass and add
them to pan.

Stir in reserved stock, 2½ tablespoons of
cream, and monkfish and season with salt
and pepper. Cover and cook very gently 10
minutes.

Trim fine skin from monkfish and add skin to
pan with bay leaf and ⅔ cup water. Simmer
20 minutes then strain and reserve stock.
Thickly slice raw bass and monkfish.

Add mullet and bass, cover, and cook an
additional 10 minutes or until fish is just
cooked. Gently stir in remaining cream and
sprinkle the top with scallions. Serve
garnished with sprigs of dill.

Makes 4 servings.

BOUILLABAISSE

2¼ lb. mixed fish fillets and shellfish, e.g. red mullet, monkfish, raw shrimp, mussels
3 tablespoons olive oil
1 onion, chopped
1 leek, sliced
1 stalk celery, chopped
2 cloves garlic, crushed
4 ripe tomatoes, peeled (see page 12) and chopped
½ teaspoon dried herbes de Provence
2 strips orange peel
large pinch saffron threads
salt and freshly ground black pepper
⅔ cup dry white wine
2⅓ cups good fish stock
chopped fresh Italian parsley, to garnish

Cut fish into chunks. Heat oil in a large saucepan. Add onion, leek, celery, and garlic and cook gently 5 minutes until soft. Add chopped tomatoes, herbes de Provence, orange peel, saffron threads, and salt and pepper. Add wine and stock and bring to a boil.

Reduce heat, add firmest fish, and simmer 5 minutes. Add more delicate fish and shellfish. Cover and simmer 5 minutes until fish is cooked through, but still retains its shape, and mussels have opened. Discard any mussels that have not opened. Garnish with chopped parsley and serve.

Makes 6 servings.

Note: Use fish and shellfish trimmings to make stock.

SQUID IN TOMATO SAUCE

1½ lb. squid
2 tablespoons olive oil
1 onion, chopped
1 clove garlic, chopped
14½ oz. can chopped tomatoes
½ cup dry white wine
1 tablespoon tomato paste
2 teaspoons chopped fresh oregano
GREMOLATA:
2 tablespoons chopped fresh parsley
grated zest 1 lemon
1 clove garlic, finely chopped

To make gremolata, mix together parsley, lemon zest, and garlic. Set aside.

To clean squid, pull head and tentacles away from body sac, bringing innards with it. Cut off tentacles and reserve. Remove ink sac. Pull transparent "quill" from body. Rinse body and tentacles and dry well. Cut body into rings and cut tentacles in half.

Heat oil in a saucepan. Add onion and garlic and cook 5 minutes until soft. Stir in tomatoes, wine, tomato paste, and oregano and season with salt and pepper. Add squid and bring to a boil. Cover and simmer 30 to 40 minutes until squid is tender. Sprinkle with gremolata and serve.

Makes 4 servings.

GREEK SEAFOOD CASSEROLE

1 tablespoon olive oil
1 onion, chopped
1 clove garlic, crushed
1 stalk celery, chopped
grated zest and juice ½ lemon
4 large ripe tomatoes, peeled (see page 12) and
  chopped
2 tablespoons chopped fresh parsley
1 fresh bay leaf
1 teaspoon dried oregano
salt and freshly ground black pepper
12 oz. monkfish fillet, skinned and diced
8 oz. squid, cleaned (see page 22) and cut into rings
1 lb. mussels, cleaned
chopped green olives, to garnish

Heat olive oil in a flameproof casserole. Add onion, garlic, and celery and cook 5 minutes until soft. Add lemon zest and juice, tomatoes, parsley, bay leaf, oregano, and salt and pepper. Bring to a boil, cover, and simmer 20 minutes. Add monkfish to the casserole, adding a little water if necessary. Return to a boil, cover and cook 3 minutes.

Stir in squid and place mussels on top. Return to a boil, cover tightly, and cook 5 minutes until fish is tender and mussels have opened. Discard any mussels that remain closed. Garnish with chopped olives and serve.

Makes 4 servings.

SQUID WITH RED WINE

1½ lb. squid
¼ cup + 3 tablespoons olive oil
1 large onion, chopped
2 cloves garlic, crushed
1 lb. tomatoes, peeled (see page 12) and roughly
  chopped
⅔ cup red wine
salt and pepper
½ teaspoon sugar
1 in. cinnamon stick
1 tablespoon chopped fresh parsley
6 slices bread, crusts removed

Clean squid (see page 22) and cut into rings. Dry thoroughly with absorbent kitchen paper. In a large saucepan, heat ¼ cup olive oil. Add onion and garlic and cook until soft. Add squid and fry until lightly browned. Add tomatoes, wine, salt, pepper, sugar, and cinnamon stick. Simmer, uncovered, 30 minutes or until squid is tender. Stir in parsley.

Sauce should be thick and rich. If not, transfer squid to a hot dish and boil sauce to reduce. Cut bread into triangles. In a skillet, heat 3 tablespoons of olive oil and fry bread until golden on both sides. Serve squid in individual dishes, with fried bread tucked round the sides.

Makes 6 servings.

COD & EGGPLANT

1 eggplant, diced
salt and freshly ground black pepper
1½ lb. thick cod fillet, cut into 4 equal pieces
5 oz. cured chorizo, skinned and thinly sliced
¼ cup olive oil
1 Spanish onion, finely chopped
2 cloves garlic, very finely chopped
1 red bell pepper, peeled, seeded, and cut into strips
1 lb. beefsteak tomatoes, peeled (see page 12),
     seeded and chopped
½ cup dry white wine
chopped fresh parsley, to garnish

Place eggplant in a colander, sprinkle with salt and leave 30 minutes. Rinse well and dry with absorbent kitchen paper. Halve each piece of cod horizontally without cutting completely in half. Open out like a book. Lay a quarter of the chorizo on one "page" of each "book", then cover with other "page". Heat oil in a flameproof casserole, add fish, and cook until evenly browned. Using a fish slice, remove fish from casserole and set aside.

Add onion to casserole and cook slowly, about 7 minutes, stirring occasionally, until soft but not colored. Stir in garlic, eggplant, and bell pepper. Cook about 4 minutes, then add tomatoes and wine and simmer about 20 minutes until vegetables are tender. Season tomato mixture and return fish to casserole. Cook an additional 10 minutes. Garnish with parsley to serve.

Makes 4 servings.

COCONUT CURRIED FISH

6 cloves garlic, chopped
1 in. piece fresh ginger, chopped
1 large fresh red chili, cored, seeded and chopped
¼ cup vegetable oil
1 large onion, quartered and sliced
2 teaspoons ground cumin
½ teaspoon ground turmeric
1¾ cups coconut milk
salt
1 lb. firm white fish fillet, such as cod or halibut, cut
     into 2 in. pieces
cilantro sprigs and lime wedges, to garnish

Put garlic, ginger, chili, and ⅔ cup water in a blender and mix until smooth.

In a wok or sauté pan over medium heat, heat oil. Add onion and fry 5 to 7 minutes until beginning to color. Add cumin and turmeric and stir 30 seconds. Stir in garlic mixture. Cook, stirring, about 2 minutes until liquid has evaporated.

Pour coconut milk into pan. Bring to a boil and bubble until sauce is reduced by half. Add salt to taste. Add fish and spoon sauce over so it is covered. Heat to a simmer and cook gently 4 to 6 minutes until fish just flakes when tested with the point of a sharp knife. Garnish with cilantro sprigs and lime wedges. Serve with rice.

Makes 3 to 4 servings.

FISH COUSCOUS

1 tablespoon vegetable oil
2 onions, chopped
8 oz. baby carrots, trimmed
8 oz. baby turnips, quartered
2 stalks celery, cut into chunks
2½ cups fish stock
salt and freshly ground black pepper
½ teaspoon saffron threads
1½ teaspoons tabil (see Note)
8 oz. baby zucchini, trimmed
1 bunch scallions
2 or 3 medium tomatoes, peeled and quartered
4 oz. shelled peas
2¼ lb. skinless cod fillet, cut into large pieces
2½ cups couscous
harissa, to serve

In a large saucepan, heat oil. Add onions and cook gently 10 minutes until soft. Add carrots, turnips, celery, and stock. Season generously with salt and pepper and add saffron and tabil. Bring to a boil, cover, and simmer 10 minutes. Add zucchini and simmer 10 minutes, then add scallions, tomatoes, and peas.

Place fish on top of vegetables, cover, and simmer 10 minutes. Meanwhile, prepare couscous as directed on the package. To serve, pile couscous in a large serving dish and arrange vegetables, then fish on top. Stir harissa, to taste, into broth and pour some over couscous. Serve with extra broth and harissa.

Makes 6 servings.

Note: Tabil is a Tunisian spice mix of coriander seeds, caraway seeds, garlic, and dried crushed chili.

SEAFOOD GUMBO

2 tablespoons olive oil
2 onions, chopped
2 cloves garlic, crushed
1 green bell pepper, seeded and chopped
1 stalk celery, chopped
2 tablespoons seasoned flour
3 cups fish stock
14½ oz. can chopped tomatoes
½ cup diced cooked ham
bouquet garni
8 oz. fresh okra, sliced
8 oz. white crabmeat, chopped
8 oz. cooked peeled shrimp
14 oz. firm white fish fillets, cut into chunks
lemon juice and Tabasco sauce, to taste
chopped fresh parsley, to garnish (optional)

In a heavy flameproof casserole, heat oil. Add onions and cook until softened. Add garlic, bell pepper, and celery and cook, stirring frequently, 5 minutes. Sprinkle over seasoned flour and stir 1 minute. Stir stock, tomatoes, ham, and bouquet garni into casserole, partially cover, and simmer 30 minutes. Add okra and simmer, covered, 30 minutes.

Add chopped fish fillets to casserole and cook about 7 minutes. Add crabmeat and shrimp and cook about 2½ minutes until shrimp are hot. Add lemon juice and Tabasco sauce to taste. Sprinkle chopped fresh parsley over the top, if desired. Serve with boiled rice.

Makes 4 to 6 servings.

SEAFOOD JAMBALAYA

2 tablespoons vegetable oil
1 lb. raw medium shrimp, shelled and deveined
8 oz. sea scallops
8 oz. pork sausage meat
1 tablespoon flour
1 large onion, chopped
3 cloves garlic, chopped
2 stalks celery, thinly sliced
1 green and 1 red bell pepper, diced
1 tablespoon Cajun seasoning mix or chili powder
1¼ cups long-grain rice
14½ oz. can chopped tomatoes
2 cups chicken stock
salt and freshly ground black pepper
1 lb. cooked crayfish tails or meat from 1 crab
chopped fresh parsley, to garnish

Heat wok until hot, add oil, and swirl to coat wok. Add shrimp and stir-fry 2 to 3 minutes, until they turn pink. Remove to a bowl. Add scallops to wok and stir-fry 2 to 3 minutes until opaque and firm. Remove scallops to bowl. Stir sausage meat into wok and stir-fry 4 to 5 minutes, until well browned. Stir flour into sausage meat until completely blended, then add onion, garlic, celery, bell peppers, and Cajun seasoning mix or chili powder. Stir-fry 4 to 5 minutes until vegetables begin to soften, then stir in rice.

Add chopped tomatoes with their liquid and chicken stock; stir well, and season with salt and freshly ground black pepper. Bring to simmering point and cook, covered, 20 minutes until rice is tender and liquid is absorbed. Stir in reserved shrimp, scallops, and cooked crayfish tails or crab pieces and cook, covered, an additional 5 minutes until seafood is heated through. Garnish with fresh parsley and serve with boiled rice.

Makes 6 servings.

SEAFOOD & RICE

2 tablespoons olive oil
1 onion, finely chopped
1 clove garlic, crushed
2 tomatoes, peeled (see page 12) and chopped
generous pinch saffron threads
1¾ cups long grain rice
2½ cups chicken stock
1 teaspoon hot pepper sauce
salt and freshly ground black pepper
1 tablespoon chopped fresh parsley
1 tablespoon chopped cilantro
1½ cups frozen peas
14 oz. package frozen seafood mixture, thawed
shrimp in shells and cilantro sprigs, to garnish

In a large pan, heat oil. Add onion and garlic and cook 10 minutes until soft. Add tomatoes, saffron, and rice and cook 5 minutes, stirring. Stir in stock, hot pepper sauce, and seasoning and bring to a boil. Lower the heat, cover, and simmer 15 minutes.

Carefully stir in parsley, cilantro, peas, and seafood. Cook, covered, 10 minutes until peas and seafood have heated through, rice is tender, and liquid has been absorbed. Add a little water if rice is too dry, or cook a little longer if all the stock has not been absorbed. Garnish with shrimp and cilantro sprigs.

Makes 4 servings.

CHICKEN & TURKEY

CHICKEN VEGETABLE HOTPOT

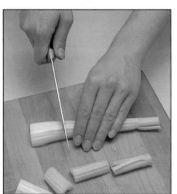

½ stick butter
4 oz. smoked bacon, chopped
2 large chicken quarters, halved
2 carrots, peeled and sliced
1 onion, sliced
2 stalks celery, cut into 2 in. lengths
2 leeks, trimmed and sliced
2 tablespoons all-purpose flour
2 lb. potatoes, peeled
2 tablespoons chopped fresh thyme
2 tablespoons chopped fresh parsley
salt and pepper
2 cups chicken stock

Preheat oven to 300F. Heat half the butter in a skillet, add bacon and chicken, and fry until golden. Remove from the pan and drain on absorbent kitchen paper to remove excess fat. Add carrots, onion, celery, and leeks to the pan and fry 2 to 3 minutes until vegetables are turning golden. Sprinkle over flour and mix well.

Slice potatoes into ¼ in. thick slices. Arrange half the slices in the bottom of a casserole, add chicken and bacon, cover with vegetables and chopped thyme and parsley, and season well with salt and pepper. Cover with remaining sliced potato, dot with remaining butter, and pour over stock. Cover and bake 1 hour, then uncover and continue cooking an additional 25 to 30 minutes until chicken is tender and cooked and potatoes are crisp and brown.

Makes 4 servings.

LENTIL-BAKED CHICKEN

1¼ cups green lentils
2 tablespoons butter
1 tablespoon olive oil
3½ lb. chicken
6 oz. smoked bacon
12 shallots, halved
4 cloves garlic, thickly sliced
⅔ cup dry white wine
1¼ cups chicken stock
1 bouquet garni
chopped fresh parsley, to garnish

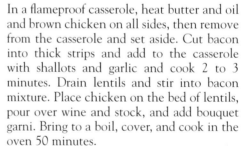

Preheat oven to 400F. Place lentils in a pan of salted water, bring to a boil, and simmer 15 minutes.

In a flameproof casserole, heat butter and oil and brown chicken on all sides, then remove from the casserole and set aside. Cut bacon into thick strips and add to the casserole with shallots and garlic and cook 2 to 3 minutes. Drain lentils and stir into bacon mixture. Place chicken on the bed of lentils, pour over wine and stock, and add bouquet garni. Bring to a boil, cover, and cook in the oven 50 minutes.

Remove the lid of the casserole, add a little water if lentil mixture is looking too dry, and return to the oven, uncovered, an additional 35 to 40 minutes until juices of the chicken run clear when pierced. Remove bouquet garni and garnish with chopped fresh parsley.

Makes 4 to 6 servings.

CHICKEN & VEGETABLES

1 tablespoon oil
4 oz. smoked bacon, chopped
2 cloves garlic, peeled
12 shallots, peeled
1 stalk celery, cut into 1 in. lengths
2 small turnips, peeled and quartered
2 carrots, peeled and cut into matchstick strips
8 oz. button mushrooms
⅔ cup dry white wine
⅔ cup chicken stock
3 lb. corn-fed chicken, without giblets
¼ cup thick cream
juice ½ lemon
salt and pepper

Preheat oven to 400F. In a flameproof casserole, heat oil. Add bacon, garlic, and shallots and fry 2 to 3 minutes. Add celery, turnips, carrots, and mushrooms and fry an additional 2 to 3 minutes until bacon is starting to turn golden brown. Pour wine over vegetables and boil rapidly to reduce liquid by half. Add chicken stock. Remove the casserole from the heat and add chicken. Cover and cook in the oven 45 to 55 minutes.

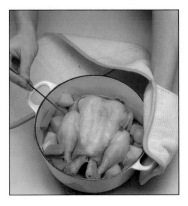

To check if chicken is cooked, pierce the leg with a skewer: it is ready if juices run clear; if not, return it to the oven to cook an additional few minutes before testing again. When cooked, remove chicken and vegetables to a serving dish. Cover and keep warm. Return the casserole to the heat, skim off any fat, and boil vigorously to reduce to just over ⅔ cup. Add cream and simmer 2 minutes; add lemon juice and salt and pepper. Serve hot with chicken.

Makes 4 servings.

COQ AU VIN

2½ cups red wine
3 cloves garlic, sliced
1 small onion, chopped
2 tablespoons olive oil
1 teaspoon brown sugar
1 teaspoon mixed peppercorns, crushed
1 teaspoon coriander seeds, crushed
1 bouquet garni
3½ lb. chicken, cut into 8 pieces
3 tablespoons seasoned flour
4 oz. piece smoked bacon, derinded and diced
6 oz. button onions, peeled
6 oz. button mushrooms
2 cups chicken stock
2 tablespoons chopped parsley
fried bread croûtons, to garnish

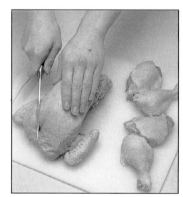

Mix together wine, garlic, chopped onion, 1 tablespoon of oil, sugar, peppercorns, and coriander seeds. Add bouquet garni and the chicken pieces. Cover and marinate in the refrigerator 2 to 3 hours, turning regularly. Remove chicken from marinade (reserving marinade) and pat dry on absorbent kitchen paper, then toss in seasoned flour. Heat remaining oil in a casserole and fry bacon until browned, remove with a slotted spoon, and set to one side. Add chicken pieces to the casserole and fry until well browned, set aside with bacon.

Add button onions and cook until browned. Add mushrooms and any remaining flour. Cook 1 minute. Add stock and marinade, stirring until thick. Return chicken and bacon, cover, and simmer 40 minutes. Remove chicken and vegetables to a serving dish using a slotted spoon; keep warm. Bring sauce to a boil and cook 3 to 4 minutes until thick. Check seasoning and stir in parsley. Spoon sauce over chicken and garnish with bread croûtons.

Makes 4 servings.

BRAISED CHICKEN WITH SPICES

4 cloves garlic, chopped
2 shallots, chopped
2 in. piece fresh ginger, chopped
1¾ cups coconut milk
2 teaspoons ground coriander
2 teaspoons ground cumin
¼ teaspoon ground turmeric
2 tablespoons vegetable oil
6 green cardamom pods
6 star anise
6 dried red chilies
1 cinnamon stick
4 cloves
20 fresh curry leaves
4 each chicken thighs and drumsticks, total weight about 2¼ lb., skinned

Put garlic, shallots, ginger, coconut milk, coriander, cumin, and turmeric into a small blender. Mix to a fine purée. In a heavy-bottomed saucepan large enough to hold chicken in a single layer, heat oil over medium heat. Add cardamom pods, star anise, chilies, cinnamon stick, cloves, and curry leaves. Fry, stirring, 2 to 3 minutes. Add ⅓ of the coconut milk mixture. Bring to boil, then add chicken pieces. Turn to coat then cook 5 minutes.

Add remaining coconut milk mixture. Bring to a simmer, then lower heat and cook gently, uncovered, 50 minutes, stirring frequently. Cook an additional 10 minutes, stirring every minute. The chicken should be golden brown and most of the milk evaporated. Pour away oily residue. Increase heat to high. Add 3 to 4 tablespoons water and stir to deglaze pan. Serve chicken with Thai rice and sauce.

Makes 4 servings.

CHICKEN IN SPICED SAUCE

2 tablespoons vegetable oil
6 each chicken thighs and drumsticks
2 lemon grass stalks, chopped
4 shallots, chopped
4 cloves garlic, chopped
2½ in. piece fresh ginger, chopped
3 tablespoons ground coriander
2 teaspoons ground turmeric
4 fresh bay leaves
1½ cups coconut milk
¼ cup Chinese chili sauce
about 2 tablespoons brown sugar, or to taste
⅓ cup roasted candlenuts or cashews, finely chopped
salt

In a large skillet over medium heat, heat oil. Add chicken and brown evenly. Transfer to absorbent kitchen paper to drain. Pour all but 1½ tablespoons of fat from the pan. Put lemon grass, shallots, garlic, and ginger in a blender and mix to a paste. Gently heat pan of fat, add spice paste, and stir 2 minutes. Stir in coriander, turmeric, and bay leaves and cook 1 minute. Stir in coconut milk, chili sauce, sugar, nuts, and salt and cook an additional minute.

Return chicken to pan and turn in sauce. Cover and cook gently 20 minutes, stirring and turning chicken frequently, until chicken juices run clear. Discard bay leaves before serving.

Makes 6 servings.

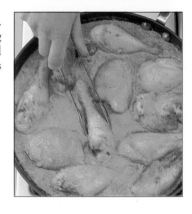

DEVIL'S CURRY

⅓ cup vegetable oil
6 shallots, thinly sliced
3 cloves garlic, thinly sliced
1 teaspoon black mustard seeds, lightly crushed
3½ lb. chicken, jointed, or small chicken portions
10 oz. small potatoes, halved
2 teaspoons mustard powder
2 tablespoons rice vinegar
1 tablespoon dark soy sauce
SPICE PASTE
10 fresh red chilies, cored, seeded and chopped
2 in. piece fresh ginger, chopped
6 shallots, chopped
3 cloves garlic, chopped
1 tablespoon ground coriander
½ teaspoon ground turmeric
8 candlenuts or cashews

To make spice paste, put chilies, ginger, chopped shallots and garlic, coriander, turmeric, and nuts in a blender and mix to a paste. In a large wok or sauté pan, heat oil over medium-high heat. Add sliced shallots and garlic and fry until lightly browned. Stir in spice paste and cook about 5 minutes, stirring. Add mustard seeds, stir once or twice, then add chicken. Cook, stirring frequently, until chicken pieces turn white.

Add potatoes and 2½ cups water. Bring to a boil, cover, then simmer 15 minutes. Stir together mustard powder, rice vinegar, and soy sauce. Stir into pan, re-cover, and cook another 15 to 20 minutes until chicken is tender, stirring occasionally.

Makes 4 to 6 servings.

AROMATIC CHICKEN

2 teaspoons tamarind paste
salt
3½ lb. chicken, cut into 10 pieces, or chicken portions, chopped
12 fresh green chilies, cored, seeded, and chopped
2 small onions, chopped
5 cloves garlic, crushed
1 ripe tomato, chopped
5 tablespoons vegetable oil
4 kaffir lime leaves
1 stalk lemon grass, crushed

Blend tamarind paste with 1 teaspoon salt and 2 tablespoons hot water. Pour mixture over chicken and rub in. Leave 1 hour.

Put chilies, onions, garlic, and tomato in a blender. Mix to a paste. In a wok or large heavy sauté pan, heat oil. Add chicken and marinade. Turn to brown on both sides then remove with a slotted spoon.

Add spice paste, lime leaves, and lemon grass to pan. Cook, stirring, 6 to 7 minutes until paste is browned. Return chicken to pan, add 1¼ cups water, and bring to a simmer. Cover and simmer gently 30 minutes until chicken juices run clear, turning chicken occasionally.

Makes 4 servings.

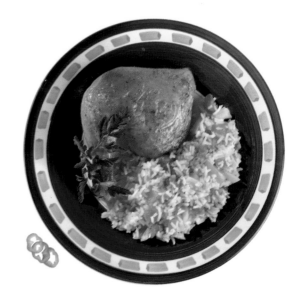

SPICY CHICKEN

2 cloves garlic, crushed
½ in. piece fresh ginger, peeled and very thinly sliced
1 tablespoon soy sauce
½ teaspoon five-spice powder
3 lb. chicken, cut into 8 pieces
2 tablespoons olive oil
2 onions, thinly sliced
1 red bell pepper, thinly sliced
8 plum tomatoes, peeled, quartered, and seeded
2 tablespoons chopped cilantro

In a large bowl, mix together garlic, ginger, soy sauce, and five-spice powder. Add chicken and turn to coat. Cover and let marinate 2 hours. Preheat oven to 350F.

Heat oil in a large flameproof casserole. Add onions and bell pepper, cover, and cook gently 10 to 15 minutes, until soft but not colored. Add tomatoes.

Add chicken and marinade, cover, and cook in the oven 25 to 30 minutes, until chicken is cooked through. Sprinkle with cilantro and serve.

Makes 4 servings.

CHILI CHICKEN WITH RICE

4 chicken joints
salt and freshly ground black pepper
⅔ cup chicken stock
⅔ cup dry white wine
1 teaspoon chili sauce
1¼ cups basmati rice
1 onion, chopped
1 yellow bell pepper, chopped
1 fresh green chili, cored, seeded, and chopped
14½ oz. can chopped tomatoes
Italian parsley sprigs, to garnish

Preheat oven to 425F. Place chicken portions in a large flameproof casserole. Season with salt and pepper.

Cook in the oven 20 minutes. Remove chicken from the casserole and keep warm. Lower oven temperature to 375F. Add stock, white wine, chili sauce, and ½ cup boiling water to the casserole. Add rice, onion, and yellow bell pepper. Stir in chopped green chili and tomatoes.

Place chicken on top of rice mixture. Cover and bake 45 minutes, until rice is tender and liquid has been absorbed. Garnish with Italian parsley and serve.

Makes 4 servings.

CHICKEN BLANQUETTE

4 slices thick-cut bacon, diced
1 tablespoon butter
1 small onion, chopped
4 chicken breast fillets
1 lb. celeriac, chopped
1 bay leaf
1 cup dry white wine or chicken stock
⅔ cup thick sour cream
salt and freshly ground black pepper

Heat a flameproof casserole, add bacon, and dry-fry until fat runs. Remove with a slotted spoon and set aside.

Heat butter in casserole, add onion, and cook, stirring occasionally, 2 to 3 minutes. Add chicken and celeriac and cook, stirring occasionally and turning chicken once or twice, 5 minutes. Add bacon, bay leaf, wine or stock, and enough water to cover. Bring to a boil, cover, and simmer gently 30 minutes, until chicken is tender.

Remove chicken, bacon, and vegetables with a slotted spoon, transfer to a warmed plate, and keep warm. Boil cooking liquid to thicken slightly. Discard bay leaf, stir in cream, return to a boil, and simmer 3 to 4 minutes. Return chicken, bacon, and vegetables to casserole, season with salt and pepper, and heat gently to warm through. Serve.

Makes 4 servings.

FLEMISH BRAISED CHICKEN

½ stick butter
4 lb. chicken
1 lb. leeks, sliced
2 or 3 carrots, sliced
½ head celery, chopped
4 oz. button mushrooms, halved
2½ cups chicken stock
2 bay leaves
12 small new potatoes
1 cup dry white wine
⅓ cup thick cream
2 egg yolks

Melt butter in a flameproof casserole. Add chicken and brown all over.

Remove from the casserole. Preheat oven to 400F. Add leeks, carrots, celery, and mushrooms to the casserole and stir well. Cover and cook 5 to 10 minutes, until soft. Add stock and bay leaves. Bring to a boil and add chicken. Cover and cook in the oven 30 minutes. Add potatoes and cook 30 minutes. Lift out chicken and remove vegetables with a slotted spoon. Keep warm.

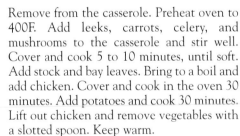

Add wine to the casserole and bring to a boil. Reduce to a simmer. In a large bowl, mix together cream and egg yolks. Pour simmering stock on to cream mixture, stirring constantly. Return to the casserole and heat gently. Do not boil. Return vegetables to the casserole. Carve chicken, garnish with parsley (if desired), and serve with vegetables and sauce.

Makes 6 servings.

MOROCCAN CHICKEN

3 cloves garlic, crushed, or 1 tablespoon garlic paste
1 teaspoon paprika
1 teaspoon ground ginger
½ teaspoon ground cumin
¼ cup olive oil
4 skinned chicken breast fillets
1 large onion, finely chopped
¼ cup chopped fresh parsley
pinch saffron threads
⅔ cup chicken stock
12 green olives
finely grated zest and juice ½ lemon

Mix garlic, paprika, ginger, and cumin with 3 tablespoons olive oil.

Place chicken portions in a shallow dish, pour over spice mix, and let marinate 3 to 4 hours. Heat remaining oil in a pan, add onion, and cook gently 2 to 3 minutes. Add chicken pieces and marinade to pan and brown chicken slightly. Add parsley, saffron, and chicken stock, cover, and simmer 30 minutes or until chicken is cooked.

Remove chicken from the pan and keep warm. Add olives and lemon zest and juice and season with a little salt and pepper. Bring to a boil and boil rapidly until reduced to approximately ⅔ cup. Pour over chicken and serve immediately.

Makes 4 servings.

BOURRIDE OF CHICKEN

2 tablespoons olive oil
3 lb. chicken, jointed into 8 pieces
4 shallots, chopped
1 leek, chopped
⅔ cup dry white wine
½ teaspoon saffron threads
cooked baby leeks, to serve
GARLIC SAUCE:
8 cloves garlic
⅔ cup mayonnaise

Heat olive oil in a flameproof casserole. Add chicken pieces and cook until browned all over. Remove with a slotted spoon and set aside.

Add shallots and leek to the casserole and cook 3 minutes until soft. Return chicken to the casserole and add wine and saffron. Bring to a boil, cover, and simmer 30 to 40 minutes until chicken is cooked through. Meanwhile, make garlic sauce. Put unpeeled garlic cloves in a small saucepan and cover with water. Bring to a boil and simmer 15 minutes until soft. Drain and let cool.

Put mayonnaise in a food processor or blender. Squeeze softened garlic out of skins into the food processor or blender. Remove chicken from the casserole and place on a warmed serving dish. Add cooking juices to the food processor or blender and quickly process. Pour over chicken. Serve with baby leeks.

Makes 4 servings.

SAFFRON CHICKEN CASSEROLE

CHICKEN TAGINE

⅔ cup dried chickpeas
½ teaspoon paprika
½ teaspoon each ground cumin and ground coriander
4½ lb. chicken, cut into serving pieces
½ stick butter
1 tablespoon vegetable oil
2 large mild onions, thinly sliced
½ teaspoon saffron threads
about 4 cups chicken stock
1 sprig thyme
¼ cup chopped fresh parsley
1¼ cups long-grain rice, to serve

Place chickpeas in a bowl. Cover with cold water and leave overnight to soak.

Drain chickpeas and place in a saucepan, cover with water, and bring to a boil. Boil 1 hour. In a bowl, mix together paprika, cumin, and coriander and add salt and pepper. Toss chicken pieces in the mixture. Heat butter and oil in a large flameproof casserole. Add chicken pieces and sauté until browned. Transfer to a plate. Add onions to the casserole and cook 10 minutes until soft. Return chicken pieces to the casserole and add chickpeas.

Add saffron threads to stock and pour over chicken to cover. Bring to a boil and add thyme. Cover and simmer gently about 1 hour or until chicken is tender. Stir in chopped parsley and check seasoning. Meanwhile, cook rice in boiling salted water about 12 minutes. To serve, drain rice and arrange half of it in a heated serving dish. Place chicken and onions on top and pour over as much saffron sauce as desired. Add remaining rice and serve with salad.

Makes 6 servings.

2 lemons
2 tablespoons vegetable oil, plus oil for frying
1 onion, chopped
3½ lb. chicken, cut into pieces
1 teaspoon ground cumin
1 teaspoon ground paprika
1 teaspoon ground ginger
large pinch saffron threads, crushed
1 cinnamon stick
salt and freshly ground black pepper
½ cup pitted green olives
peel from 1 preserved lemon, cut into strips
2 tablespoons chopped cilantro
1 tablespoon chopped fresh parsley
harissa, to serve

With a zester, remove zest from lemons and place in a bowl. Squeeze juice over and set aside. In a heavy-bottomed casserole, heat oil. Add onion and cook 10 minutes until soft. Remove onion and add chicken pieces. Cook until browned all over. Stir in cumin, paprika, ginger, saffron, and cinnamon stick. Cook 1 minute then return onions to the casserole. Pour in 1 cup water. Season with salt and pepper and bring to a boil. Cover and simmer gently 45 minutes.

Stir in olives, preserved lemon peel, cilantro, and parsley and cook and additional 10 to 15 minutes until chicken is cooked. Meanwhile, drain lemon zest and pat dry with absorbent kitchen paper. In a small saucepan, heat ½ in. oil. Add zest, which will crisp almost immediately. Quickly drain off oil through a strainer. Serve chicken and sauce with fried lemon zest scattered over. Serve with bread, with harissa handed separately.

Makes 6 servings.

POULET PROVENÇAL

10 cloves garlic
1 tablespoon finely chopped fresh thyme
1 tablespoon finely chopped fresh marjoram
salt and freshly ground black pepper
3½ lb. chicken, cut into 8 pieces
2 tablespoons lemon juice
¼ cup olive oil
1 small sprig rosemary
1 sprig thyme
6 basil leaves, shredded
8 anchovy fillets, drained and chopped
4 beefsteak tomatoes, peeled (see page 12), seeded,
  and chopped
⅔ cup dry white wine
24 Niçoise olives
chopped fresh herbs and basil sprigs, to garnish

Crush two garlic cloves and mix with chopped fresh thyme and marjoram and a small pinch of salt. Cut small incisions in chicken pieces and insert a little herb mixture into each incision. Rub chicken with lemon juice and pepper and let stand in a cool place 2 hours. Preheat oven to 325F. Heat half the oil in a saucepan. Finely chop remaining garlic and add to pan with rosemary, thyme, and basil. Cook, stirring occasionally, 5 minutes. Stir in anchovy fillets, tomatoes, wine, and bell pepper. Bring to a boil and simmer 15 minutes.

Heat remaining oil in a heavy, flameproof casserole, add chicken, and cook until browned all over. Pour over sauce, cover, and cook in the oven 45 minutes, turning chicken once or twice. Add olives and cook an additional 15 minutes. Garnish with mixed fresh herbs and basil sprigs and serve.

Makes 4 servings.

Note: Niçoise olives have a special flavor as they are marinated in oil and herbs. If they are not available, use plain black olives.

CIDER APPLE CHICKEN

pared peel from 1 lemon plus 1 teaspoon juice
½ cinnamon stick
1 onion, quartered
3½ lb. chicken
salt and pepper
¾ stick butter
1 tablespoon oil
3 tablespoons brandy
4 eating apples, peeled and cored
⅔ cup cider
1¼ cups thick sour cream
1 tablespoon each chopped fresh chives and parsley

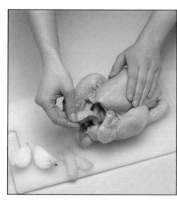

Place lemon peel, cinnamon stick, and onion inside chicken. Season well.

Preheat oven to 350F. In a flameproof casserole, heat ½ stick butter and oil and brown chicken on all sides. Pour over brandy and ignite. Thinly slice one of the apples and add to the casserole once the flames have died down. Add cider to the casserole, bring to a boil, cover, and cook in the oven 1¼ hours.

Melt remaining butter in a pan, cut remaining apples into thick slices, and sauté until just cooked. Remove chicken from the casserole, place on a warmed serving platter, and surround with sautéed apples. Add thick sour cream and lemon juice to the casserole, stir well, and boil to reduce slightly. Season well and pour over chicken. Sprinkle with chopped chives and parsley and serve.

Makes 4 to 6 servings.

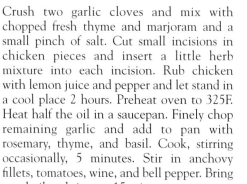

CHICKEN PUTTANESCA

¼ cup olive oil
1 red onion, chopped
2 cloves garlic, crushed
2 oz. can anchovies in olive oil, drained
9 black olives, pitted
¼ cup sun-dried tomatoes
14½ oz. can chopped tomatoes
½ teaspoon crushed dried chilies
2 teaspoons chopped fresh oregano
1 tablespoon balsamic vinegar
8 skinless, boneless chicken thighs
oregano sprigs, to garnish

Heat half the oil in a large saucepan. Add onion and garlic and cook 5 minutes.

Chop anchovies, olives, and sun-dried tomatoes. Add to the pan with tomatoes, chilies, oregano, balsamic vinegar, and salt and pepper. Bring to a boil. Heat remaining oil in a large skillet. Add chicken and cook until browned all over.

Remove with a slotted spoon and add to the saucepan. Turn to coat with sauce. Cover and simmer 30 minutes or until chicken is cooked through. Garnish with oregano sprigs and serve.

Makes 4 servings.

BURGUNDY CHICKEN

2 tablespoons butter
4 chicken legs
1 shallot, finely chopped
2 tablespoons Marc de Bourgogne or brandy
1 cup white Burgundy or other Chardonnay wine
2 sprigs thyme
salt and freshly ground black pepper
1 cup seedless green grapes, halved
¼ cup thick cream
Italian parsley and thyme sprigs, to garnish

Heat butter in a heavy flameproof casserole, add chicken, and cook until browned all over. Remove and drain on kitchen paper.

Add shallot to casserole and cook, stirring occasionally, 2 to 3 minutes, until soft. Return chicken to casserole. Pour over marc de Bourgogne or brandy and ignite. When flames have died down, add wine, thyme, and salt and pepper.

Bring to a boil, cover, and simmer very gently, turning chicken two or three times, 50 to 60 minutes. Transfer chicken to warmed serving plates and keep warm. Add grapes to casserole and boil until sauce is thickened slightly. Stir in cream and simmer to thicken slightly. Pour over chicken, garnish with Italian parsley and thyme, and serve.

Makes 4 servings.

SUGARED CHICKEN CASSEROLE

8 chicken thighs
3 tablespoons oil
2 teaspoons sugar
1 onion, finely chopped
2 stalks celery, chopped
½ cup chicken stock
2 large plum tomatoes, peeled, seeded, and chopped
8 oz. okra
MARINADE:
1 red onion, roughly chopped
2 cloves garlic, roughly chopped
1 in. piece fresh ginger, chopped
1 red chili, seeded and roughly chopped
2 tablespoons chopped cilantro
1 tablespoon olive oil
juice ½ lime

To make marinade, put onion, garlic, ginger, chili, cilantro, olive oil, lime juice, and seasoning in a blender or food processor and process to a paste. Rub over chicken thighs and place in a dish. Cover and refrigerate overnight. Scrape marinade off chicken and reserve. Dry chicken thighs on absorbent kitchen paper. In a skillet, heat oil. Add sugar and cook gently until sugar dissolves. Add chicken and cook, turning frequently, until well browned. Transfer to a casserole.

Add onion and celery to oil in skillet and cook 10 minutes until soft. Stir chicken stock into pan, scraping up any sediment, then pour over chicken. Bring to a boil, then cover and simmer gently 20 minutes. Add tomatoes and okra and cook an additional 15 minutes. Add 2 or 3 tablespoons of reserved marinade, according to taste. Season and serve.

Makes 4 servings.

CHICKEN WITH MUSHROOMS

1 tablespoon olive oil
1 tablespoon unsalted butter, diced
4 chicken quarters
12 oz. chestnut, oyster, shiitake or chanterelle
  mushrooms, or a mixture
1 onion, finely chopped
¾ cup medium-dry white wine
2 tablespoons chopped fresh tarragon leaves
½ cup plain yogurt
salt and freshly ground black pepper
tarragon sprigs, to garnish

Heat oil and butter in a heavy flameproof casserole, add chicken, and cook until browned. Remove with a slotted spoon.

Preheat oven to 325F. Cut large mushrooms into quarters and oyster mushrooms into 1 in. strips. Add to casserole with onion and cook, stirring occasionally, 5 minutes, until soft. Stir in wine and bring to a boil. Return chicken to casserole and sprinkle with tarragon. Cover tightly and cook in the oven 1 hour.

Using a slotted spoon, transfer chicken and vegetables to a warmed plate and keep warm. Boil cooking liquid to thicken slightly. Stir in yogurt and reheat gently without boiling. Season with salt and pepper. Return chicken and vegetables to casserole, turn in sauce, and heat gently to warm through. Garnish with tarragon sprigs and serve.

Makes 4 servings.

CHICKEN PELAU

1 onion, roughly chopped
2 cloves garlic
2 stalks celery, roughly chopped
2 tablespoons chopped fresh chives
1 tablespoon fresh thyme leaves
liquid from 1 fresh coconut
flesh from ½ fresh coconut, chopped
1 Scotch bonnet chili
2 tablespoons oil
3¾ lb. chicken, cut into 2 in. pieces
15 oz. can gungo peas, drained
1¼ cups long-grain rice, washed
1⅓ cups chicken stock
salt and freshly ground black pepper
12 pimento-stuffed olives, halved, to garnish

Place onion, garlic, celery, chives, and thyme in a blender or food processor with ¼ cup water and process to a paste. Transfer to a saucepan. Put coconut liquid and coconut flesh in the blender or food processor and blend until it will coat the back of a spoon. Add water if too thick. Stir into onion mixture with chili and cook gently 15 minutes.

Put oil and sugar in a wide-bottomed, flameproof casserole. Heat gently until sugar begins to caramelize. Add chicken pieces and cook 20 minutes, turning frequently, until well browned. Stir in coconut mixture, gungo peas, rice, and stock. Season and bring to a boil; cover, and simmer 20 minutes until chicken is tender, rice is cooked, and liquid has been absorbed. Remove and discard chili. Garnish with halved pimento-stuffed olives and serve.

Makes 6 servings.

MEXICALI CHICKEN

2 tablespoons sunflower oil
1 medium sized onion, chopped
1 small fresh green chili, seeded and chopped
1 clove garlic, finely chopped
2 tablespoons tomato paste
1 teaspoon ground cumin
1 tablespoon finely chopped cilantro
1 cup cooked red kidney beans
1 lb. tomatoes, peeled (see page 12) and chopped
3 cups cooked, diced chicken
salt and pepper

Heat oil in a heavy-bottomed saucepan and fry onion, chili, and garlic over medium heat 4 to 5 minutes until onion is soft but not brown.

Stir in tomato paste, cumin, cilantro, kidney beans, tomatoes, and chicken; season with salt and pepper. Cover and simmer 20 minutes until thick; if necessary, uncover and simmer an additional 10 minutes. Serve with boiled rice or tortillas and a salad.

Makes 4 servings.

CHICKEN CHASSEUR

1 tablespoon olive oil
3 tablespoons butter
4 chicken quarters
3 shallots, finely chopped
1 clove garlic, finely chopped
1 tablespoon all-purpose flour
5 oz. brown cap or shiitake mushrooms, sliced
1 cup dry white wine
2 beefsteak tomatoes, peeled, seeded, and chopped
several sprigs tarragon and parsley
tarragon sprigs, to garnish

Heat oil and 2 tablespoons butter in a heavy flameproof casserole, add chicken, and cook until browned all over.

Remove chicken and set aside. Add shallots and garlic to casserole and cook, stirring occasionally, 5 minutes, until soft. Add flour and mushrooms and cook, stirring until flour has browned lightly. Stir in wine and tomatoes. Bring to a boil, stirring.

Return chicken to casserole and add tarragon, parsley, salt, and pepper. Cover tightly and cook gently 50 to 60 minutes. Remove chicken with a slotted spoon, transfer to warmed serving plates and keep warm. Remove herbs from sauce and discard. Boil sauce to thicken slightly. Lower heat and stir in remaining butter. Pour sauce over chicken, garnish with tarragon sprigs, and serve.

Makes 4 servings.

POULET BASQUAISE

3 red bell peppers
3 lb. chicken, cut into 8 pieces
salt and freshly ground black pepper
3 tablespoons olive oil
2 onions, thinly sliced
3 cloves garlic, chopped
½ fresh red chili, cored, seeded, and chopped
4 ripe tomatoes, peeled, seeded, and chopped
bouquet garni
4 oz. Bayonne or Parma ham, diced
½ cup dry white wine
chopped fresh parsley, to garnish

Preheat broiler. Broil bell peppers until charred and blistered all over.

Leave peppers until cool enough to handle, then peel. Halve, remove cores and seeds, and cut flesh into strips. Season chicken with salt and pepper. Heat oil in a heavy flameproof casserole, add chicken, and cook until browned all over. Remove with tongs or a slotted spoon, transfer to a large plate, and set aside.

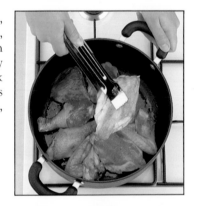

Add onions and garlic to casserole and cook, stirring occasionally, 5 minutes, until soft. Stir in chili, tomatoes, and bouquet garni and simmer 15 minutes. Stir in ham, wine, and peppers. Bring to a boil, add chicken and any juices on plate, and season with pepper. Cover tightly and simmer gently 50 to 60 minutes. Transfer chicken to warmed serving plates. Boil sauce to thicken, pour over chicken, garnish with chopped parsley, and serve.

Makes 4 servings.

LEMON CHICKEN

½ stick butter
3½ lb. chicken quarters
16 button onions
1 cup chicken stock
1 cup dry white wine
bouquet garni
salt and freshly ground black pepper
12 button mushrooms, quartered
2 large egg yolks, lightly beaten
juice ½ lemon
chopped fresh parsley, to garnish

Heat butter in a heavy flameproof casserole, add chicken pieces and onions, and cook 10 minutes, until chicken is browned.

Remove onions with a slotted spoon and set aside. Add stock, wine, bouquet garni, and salt and pepper. Bring to a boil, cover, and simmer 20 minutes. Return onions to casserole and cook 20 minutes. Add mushrooms and cook 10 minutes.

Using a slotted spoon, transfer chicken and vegetables to a warmed plate, cover, and keep warm. Boil cooking liquid until reduced by one-third. Remove a ladleful of cooking liquid, allow to cool slightly, then stir into egg yolks. Reduce heat, stir egg yolk mixture into casserole, and heat very gently, stirring, until slightly thickened: do not boil. Stir in lemon juice. Return chicken and vegetables to casserole and turn in sauce. Garnish with parsley and serve.

Makes 4 servings.

BRAISED CHICKEN

3½ lb. chicken
1 onion, halved
2 cloves
4 oz. bacon, chopped (optional)
about 4 cups stock or water
bouquet garni
salt and freshly ground black pepper
4 stalks celery, quartered
4 carrots, quartered
4 small turnips, quartered
12 small leeks, halved
bay leaves, to garnish

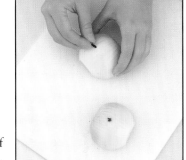

Put chicken into a large heavy flameproof casserole. Stud each onion half with 1 clove.

Add onion halves to casserole with bacon, if using. Add enough stock or water to cover and bring to a boil. Add bouquet garni and salt and pepper. Skim scum from surface, cover, and simmer very gently 1 hour.

Add celery, carrots, and turnips, cover, and cook 30 minutes. Add leeks and cook 15 minutes, until chicken and vegetables are tender. Transfer chicken and vegetables to a warmed serving plate and keep warm. Boil sauce to thicken slightly. Carve chicken and serve with vegetables and sauce, garnished with bay leaves.

Makes 4 servings.

LEMON & CILANTRO CHICKEN

4 chicken thighs, skinned
4 chicken drumsticks, skinned
¼ cup vegetable oil
2 in. piece fresh ginger, grated
4 cloves garlic, crushed
1 fresh green chili, seeded and finely chopped
½ teaspoon turmeric
1 teaspoon ground cumin
1 teaspoon ground coriander
salt and cayenne pepper
grated zest and juice 1 lemon
3 cups chopped cilantro leaves
cilantro leaves and lemon slices, to garnish

Wash chicken joints and pat dry with absorbent kitchen paper. Heat oil in a large skillet, add chicken, and fry, stirring frequently, until browned all over. Remove from pan with a slotted spoon and set aside. Add ginger and garlic to pan and fry 1 minute. Stir in chili, turmeric, cumin, and ground coriander and season with salt and cayenne pepper, then cook 1 minute.

Return chicken to pan, add ½ cup water and lemon zest and juice. Bring to a boil, then cover and cook over a medium heat 25 to 30 minutes, or until chicken is tender. Stir in chopped cilantro, then serve hot, garnished with cilantro leaves and lemon slices.

Makes 4 servings.

Variation: Use fresh parsley, or parsley and mint, instead of cilantro, if preferred.

CHICKEN GUMBO

2 tablespoons butter
1 tablespoon oil
3½ lb. chicken, cut into 8 pieces
¼ cup seasoned flour
1 large onion, sliced
2 cloves garlic, sliced
2 teaspoons chili powder
14½ oz. can chopped tomatoes
2 tablespoons tomato paste
1¼ cups chicken stock
½ cup red wine
1 red bell pepper, seeded and sliced
1 green bell pepper, seeded and sliced
12 oz. small okra, trimmed
2 teaspoons lemon juice
pinch sugar

Preheat oven to 350F. Heat butter and oil in a flameproof casserole. Toss chicken pieces in seasoned flour, then fry in the hot fats until golden. Remove from the pan and set aside. Cook onion and garlic in the casserole until slightly softened, stir in chili powder and any remaining flour, then add tomatoes, tomato paste, stock, and wine and bring to a boil.

Stir in red and green bell pepper, okra, lemon juice, and sugar and return chicken to the casserole. Cover and cook in the oven 50 to 60 minutes. Serve with rice, if desired.

Makes 4 servings.

CHICKEN BIRYANI

½ cup vegetable oil
1 stick cinnamon
8 cloves
6 cardamom pods, bruised
1 in. piece fresh ginger, finely chopped
1½ lb. skinned and boned chicken, diced
2 cloves garlic, crushed
1 teaspoon chili powder
1¼ cups plain yogurt
⅔ cup chicken stock
pinch saffron threads
¼ cup boiling water
1¾ cups basmati rice
¼ cup golden raisins
¼ cup slivered almonds
1 onion, sliced

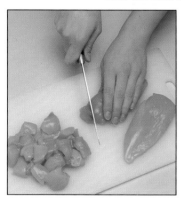

Preheat oven to 375F. In a flameproof casserole, heat ¼ cup oil. Add cinnamon stick, cloves, cardamom pods, and ginger and fry 15 seconds. Add chicken, garlic, and chili and fry 4 minutes. Add yogurt, 1 tablespoon at a time, stirring between each addition until yogurt is absorbed by the spices. Add stock and simmer 20 to 25 minutes. Transfer to a bowl. Soak saffron in boiling water and put to one side. Wash rice under cold running water until water runs clear, then cook in boiling, salted water 3 minutes and drain.

Put 2 tablespoons oil in the casserole, spoon in a layer of rice, sprinkle with a little of the saffron water, and cover with a layer of chicken. Repeat, ending with a layer of rice. Add any cooking juices left from the chicken, cover tightly, and cook in the oven 25 to 30 minutes. In a pan, heat remaining oil and fry golden raisins and almonds until golden; remove. Fry onions until crisp and golden. Sprinkle the biryani with almonds, onions, and golden raisins.

Makes 4 servings.

APRICOT & CHICKEN CURRY

2½ lb. chicken joints, skinned
½ teaspoon chili powder
1 tablespoon garam masala
1 in. piece fresh ginger, grated
2 cloves garlic, crushed
1 cup ready-to-eat dried apricots
2 tablespoons vegetable oil
2 onions, finely sliced
14½ oz. can chopped tomatoes
1 tablespoon sugar
2 tablespoons white wine vinegar
salt

Wash chicken and pat dry with absorbent kitchen paper. Cut each joint into 4 pieces and put in a large bowl. Add chili powder, garam masala, ginger, and garlic and toss well to coat chicken pieces. Cover and leave in a cool place 2 to 3 hours, to allow chicken to absorb flavors. In a separate bowl, put apricots and ⅔ cup water and let soak 2 to 3 hours.

Heat oil in a large heavy-bottomed pan and add chicken. Fry over a high heat 5 minutes or until browned all over. Remove from pan and set aside. Add onions to pan and cook, stirring, about 5 minutes, until soft. Return chicken to pan with tomatoes and cook, covered, over a low heat 20 minutes. Drain apricots, add to pan with sugar and vinegar. Season with salt. Simmer, covered, 10 to 15 minutes. Serve hot.

Makes 4 servings.

SPICY SPANISH CHICKEN

¼ cup olive oil
4 slices day-old French bread
8 cloves garlic
3½ lb. chicken, skinned and cut into small pieces
1¼ cups medium-bodied dry white wine
large pinch saffron threads, finely crushed
3 tablespoons chopped fresh parsley
3 cloves
freshly grated nutmeg
salt and freshly ground black pepper

Heat oil in a flameproof casserole, add bread and 5 garlic cloves, and fry until browned.

Transfer to a mortar and crush with a pestle, then transfer to a bowl. Crush remaining garlic and add to casserole with chicken. Cook until chicken changes color. Pour in wine and just enough water to cover chicken. Cover casserole and simmer gently about 30 minutes until chicken juices run clear when thickest part is pierced with a sharp knife.

Meanwhile, in a bowl, dissolve saffron in 2 tablespoons of the chicken cooking liquid. Put parsley, cloves, and nutmeg in the mortar and pound to a paste. Stir in saffron. Mix with crushed bread, then stir mixture into the casserole and cook 10 minutes. Season to taste and serve.

Makes 4 servings.

CHICKEN WITH SHERRY

¼ cup raisins
1 cup oloroso sherry
3 tablespoons olive oil
3½ lb. chicken, cut into 8 pieces
1 Spanish onion, finely chopped
1 clove garlic, finely chopped
1 cup chicken stock
salt and freshly ground black pepper
¼ cup pine nuts

In a small bowl, soak raisins in sherry 30 minutes.

In a flameproof casserole, heat 2 tablespoons oil, add chicken, and cook gently until lightly and evenly browned, about 10 minutes. Transfer to absorbent kitchen paper to drain. Add onion and garlic to casserole and cook gently, stirring occasionally, until softened and lightly colored, about 7 minutes. Strain raisins and set aside.

Stir sherry into casserole. Simmer until reduced by half. Add stock, chicken, and seasoning, bring to a boil, then simmer gently about 35 minutes, until chicken is cooked. In a small pan, fry pine nuts in remaining oil until lightly colored. Drain on absorbent kitchen paper, then stir into casserole with raisins. Transfer chicken to a warm serving dish. Boil liquid in casserole to concentrate slightly. Pour over chicken.

Makes 4 servings.

CHICKEN IN VINEGAR SAUCE

4 chicken breast fillets
salt and freshly ground black pepper
⅓ cup olive oil
12 cloves garlic
1 small onion, finely chopped
about 3 tablespoons sherry vinegar
1 tablespoon paprika
1½ tablespoons chopped fresh oregano
2 tablespoons fresh breadcrumbs
1¼ cups chicken stock
fresh herbs, to garnish

Season chicken with salt and pepper. Heat oil in a heavy flameproof casserole, add chicken, and cook 10 minutes.

Meanwhile, slice 4 of the garlic cloves. Add sliced garlic to casserole with onion and cook until chicken is lightly browned all over, about an additional 5 minutes.

Remove chicken from casserole, stir in vinegar, and boil 2 to 3 minutes. Pound remaining garlic with a little salt, paprika, and oregano, then stir in breadcrumbs and a quarter of the stock. Pour over chicken, add remaining stock, and cook about 20 minutes, until chicken is tender and sauce fairly thick. Adjust seasoning and amount of vinegar, if necessary. Serve garnished with fresh herbs.

Makes 4 servings.

CHICKEN PEPITORIA

2 tablespoons olive oil
3½ lb. chicken, cut into 8 pieces, or 4 large chicken
  portions, halved
½ Spanish onion, finely chopped
4 oz. serrano ham, cut into strips
1 cup chicken stock
4 cloves garlic, crushed
15 almonds or hazelnuts, lightly roasted
pinch ground cloves
3 tablespoons chopped fresh parsley
3 egg yolks
salt and freshly ground black pepper

Heat oil in a flameproof casserole, add chicken and fry until lightly browned all over. Using a slotted spoon, remove chicken from casserole and set aside. Add onion to casserole and cook about 4 minutes, stirring occasionally. Stir in ham, cook 1 minute, then return chicken to casserole. Pour in stock, cover tightly and simmer gently about 45 minutes until chicken is tender.

Meanwhile, pound together garlic, almonds or hazelnuts, ground cloves, and parsley. Place in a small bowl and gradually work in egg yolks. Stir a little hot chicken liquid into the bowl, then stir mixture into the casserole. Continue to cook gently, stirring, until sauce thickens; do not allow to boil. Season with salt and pepper.

Makes 4 servings.

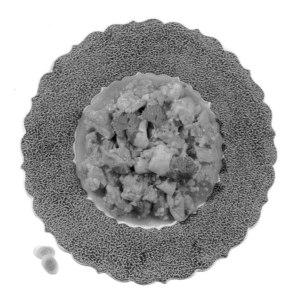

MALAYSIAN SPICED CHICKEN

MUGHLAI CHICKEN

8 chicken thighs, boned and chopped
3 tablespoons vegetable oil
1 clove garlic, finely chopped
2 tablespoons fish sauce
6 shallots, finely chopped
cilantro leaves, to garnish
MARINADE
2 small fresh red chilies, cored, seeded, and chopped
1 stalk lemon grass, chopped
1 clove garlic, crushed
1½ in. piece fresh ginger, chopped
1 tablespoon ground turmeric
1 cup canned tomatoes
1 tablespoon light brown sugar
salt

6 cloves garlic, peeled
½ cup blanched almonds
1 in. piece ginger, peeled and chopped
⅓ cup vegetable oil
2¼ lb. chicken pieces, diced
9 whole cardamom pods
1 stick cinnamon
6 whole cloves
1 onion, finely chopped
2½ teaspoons ground cumin
1 teaspoon cayenne pepper
⅔ cup plain yogurt
1¼ cups thick cream
1 tablespoon golden raisins
1 firm, ripe banana
½ teaspoon each garam masala and salt

To make marinade, put chilies, lemon grass, garlic, ginger, turmeric, tomatoes, sugar, and salt in a blender and mix together well. Put chicken in a non-reactive bowl and pour marinade over. Stir together, cover, and refrigerate overnight. Return bowl of chicken to room temperature 1 hour. In a wok or heavy sauté pan, heat oil over high heat. Add garlic and fry 30 seconds. Add chicken and marinade. Stir and toss together, then stir in fish sauce and ¼ cup hot water. Cover, lower heat, and simmer 5 minutes.

Put garlic, almonds, ginger, and ¼ cup water into a blender and blend to form a paste. Heat oil in a flameproof casserole or saucepan and fry chicken until golden. Set aside. Put cardamom, cinnamon, and cloves into the pan and fry a few seconds. Add chopped onion and fry until beginning to turn golden brown. Add paste from the blender together with cumin and cayenne pepper and fry 2 minutes, or until mixture is lightly browned.

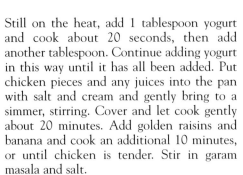

Add shallots and continue to cook, uncovered, stirring occasionally, about 10 minutes, until chicken juices run clear. Serve garnished with cilantro.

Makes 4 servings.

Still on the heat, add 1 tablespoon yogurt and cook about 20 seconds, then add another tablespoon. Continue adding yogurt in this way until it has all been added. Put chicken pieces and any juices into the pan with salt and cream and gently bring to a simmer, stirring. Cover and let cook gently about 20 minutes. Add golden raisins and banana and cook an additional 10 minutes, or until chicken is tender. Stir in garam masala and salt.

Makes 4 servings.

THAI CHICKEN CURRY

1 small onion, chopped
1 clove garlic, peeled
1 stalk lemon grass, chopped
1 teaspoon ground coriander
½ teaspoon dried chili flakes
1 teaspoon grated lime zest
1 teaspoon paprika
½ teaspoon ground cumin
2 teaspoons vegetable oil
1 lb. raw chicken meat, sliced
1 tablespoon light soy sauce
⅔ cup coconut milk
2 lime leaves
¼ cup chicken stock
2 red bell peppers, seeded and sliced
10 scallions, sliced into matchstick strips

Blend or process onion, garlic, lemon grass, ground coriander, dried chili flakes, lime zest, paprika, and cumin in a blender or food processor until smooth. Heat oil in a large skillet, stir in paste, and cook 1 to 2 minutes. Add chicken and stir gently, coating well in curry paste.

Stir in soy sauce, coconut milk, lime leaves, chicken stock, bell peppers, and scallions. Cover and cook 20 to 25 minutes. Serve with plain boiled rice and garnish with sprigs of cilantro.

Makes 4 servings.

CHICKEN & PLUM CASSEROLE

1 oz. dried Chinese mushrooms, soaked in hot water 20 minutes
1 lb. skinless, boneless chicken thighs
1 tablespoon sunflower oil
2 cloves garlic, thinly sliced
1 oz. Prosciutto, trimmed and diced
4 or 5 plums, halved and pitted
1 tablespoon brown sugar
3 tablespoons light soy sauce
2 tablespoons rice wine
3 tablespoons plum sauce
1 tablespoon chili sauce
2½ cups chicken stock
2 teaspoons cornstarch mixed with 4 teaspoons water

Drain mushrooms and squeeze out excess water. Discard mushroom stems and thinly slice caps. Trim fat from chicken thighs and cut meat into 1 in. strips. Heat oil in a nonstick or well-seasoned wok and stir-fry chicken, garlic, and Prosciutto 3 to 4 minutes. Add mushrooms and stir-fry 1 minute.

Add plums, brown sugar, soy sauce, rice wine, plum sauce, and chili sauce and simmer 20 minutes or until plums have softened. Add cornstarch mixture, and cook, stirring, until thickened. Serve on a bed of rice.

Makes 4 servings.

CHICKEN IN SANFAINA SAUCE

¼ cup olive oil
3 lb. chicken, cut into 8 pieces
2 Spanish onions, chopped
2 cloves garlic, chopped
1 green bell pepper, seeded and sliced
1 red bell pepper, seeded and sliced
2 eggplants, cut into strips
4 oz. serrano ham, diced
1 lb. beefsteak tomatoes, peeled (see page 12),
    seeded, and chopped
½ cup dry white wine
½ cup chicken stock
bouquet garni of 1 bay leaf, 1 sprig thyme and 1
    sprig parsley
salt and freshly ground black pepper
1 tablespoon chopped fresh parsley, to garnish

Heat oil in a large, heavy flameproof casserole, add chicken, and fry about 10 minutes until lightly browned. Using a slotted spoon, remove chicken and reserve. Add onions and garlic to casserole and fry 1 minute. Add bell peppers and eggplants and cook, stirring occasionally, 5 minutes. Stir in ham, tomatoes, wine, stock, bouquet garni, and salt and pepper.

Bring casserole to a boil, then reduce heat so liquid barely simmers. Return chicken to casserole and bury in sauce. Cover casserole and cook gently about 45 minutes, until chicken juices run clear when pierced with a sharp knife and sauce is slightly thickened. Discard bouquet garni. Taste and adjust seasoning. Serve sprinkled with parsley.

Makes 4 servings.

Note: Use 4 large chicken portions, halved, instead of whole chicken, if preferred.

POULET AU VINAIGRE

1 tablespoon oil
1 tablespoon) butter
4 chicken legs
1 onion, finely chopped
bouquet garni
4 ripe tomatoes, peeled, seeded, and chopped
2 teaspoons tomato paste
1¼ cups red wine vinegar
1¼ cups chicken stock
salt and freshly ground black pepper
chopped fresh parsley, to garnish

Heat oil and butter in a heavy flameproof casserole. Add chicken and cook until lightly browned all over.

Remove chicken and set aside. Add onion to casserole and cook, stirring occasionally, 5 minutes, until soft. Return chicken to casserole, add bouquet garni, cover, and cook gently 20 minutes, turning occasionally.

Add tomatoes to casserole, and cook, uncovered, until liquid has evaporated. Combine tomato paste and vinegar and add to casserole. Simmer until most of liquid has evaporated. Add stock and salt and pepper and simmer until reduced by half. Sprinkle with parsley and serve.

Makes 4 servings.

CACCIATORE

2 tablespoons olive oil
4 large chicken breasts, with bones
1 large or 2 small red onions, thinly sliced
2 cloves garlic, thinly sliced
⅔ cup red wine
⅔ cup chicken stock
14½ oz. can chopped tomatoes
1 tablespoon tomato paste
1 red bell pepper, seeded and sliced
1 yellow bell pepper, seeded and sliced
2 tablespoons chopped fresh basil
salt and pepper
pinch sugar
pasta noodles, to serve

Preheat oven to 350F. In a pan, heat oil and fry chicken breasts all over until golden brown, then transfer to a shallow casserole. Gently fry onion and garlic in the pan without browning. Add wine, stock, tomatoes, tomato paste, bell peppers, 1 tablespoon of the basil, salt and pepper, and sugar and bring to a boil.

Pour sauce over chicken, cover, and cook in the oven 45 minutes. Serve on a bed of pasta noodles and sprinkle with remaining basil and plenty of black pepper.

Makes 4 servings.

CHICKEN WITH PARSLEY

3 tablespoons olive oil
3½ lb. chicken, cut into 8 pieces
3 cloves garlic, lightly crushed
½ fresh red chili, seeded and finely chopped
⅓ cup dry white wine
salt and freshly ground black pepper
juice ½ lemon
3 tablespoons chopped fresh parsley

Heat oil in a flameproof casserole; add chicken and cook about 10 minutes until lightly browned. Cook in batches, if necessary. Remove and reserve.

Add garlic and chili to casserole and cook 5 minutes without browning, stirring occasionally. Return chicken to casserole, pour wine over it, and allow to bubble 2 to 3 minutes.

Season lightly, cover, and cook gently about 40 minutes until chicken juices run clear when pierced with a sharp knife. Transfer chicken to a warm plate and keep warm. Stir lemon juice and parsley into casserole. Boil if necessary to lightly concentrate juices, then pour it over chicken.

Makes 4 servings.

Note: Use 4 large chicken portions, halved, instead of whole chicken, if preferred.

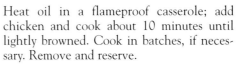

TURKEY KORMA

1 teaspoon turmeric
1 teaspoon ground cumin
1 teaspoon ground coriander
½ teaspoon ground ginger
⅔ cup plain yogurt
2 teaspoons lemon juice
½ cup coconut milk
½ cup chicken stock
1 cup unsweetened dried coconut
3 cups diced cooked turkey meat
cilantro sprigs, to garnish

Preheat oven to 375F. Dry-fry turmeric, cumin, coriander, and ginger in a flameproof casserole 2 to 3 minutes.

Add yogurt, lemon juice, coconut milk, stock, dried coconut, and salt and pepper and mix well. Stir in turkey.

Bring to a boil, cover, and cook in the oven 30 to 40 minutes. Garnish with cilantro sprigs and serve with rice.

Makes 4 servings.

GINGER TURKEY & CABBAGE

1¼ cups red wine
2 tablespoons red wine vinegar
⅔ cup golden raisins
2 cups ready-to-eat dried apricots, halved
1 in. piece fresh ginger, peeled and grated
2 cloves garlic, crushed
salt and freshly ground black pepper
4 x 6 oz. turkey fillets
½ red cabbage, shredded
Italian parsley sprigs, to garnish

In a large bowl, mix together red wine, vinegar, golden raisins, apricots, ginger, garlic, and salt and pepper. Add turkey.

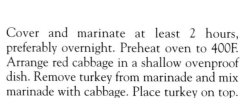

Cover and marinate at least 2 hours, preferably overnight. Preheat oven to 400F. Arrange red cabbage in a shallow ovenproof dish. Remove turkey from marinade and mix marinade with cabbage. Place turkey on top.

Cook in the oven 45 to 50 minutes, until turkey is tender and cooked through. Garnish with Italian parsley and serve.

Makes 4 servings.

DUCK & GAME

DUCK WITH APPLES & PRUNES

MEDITERRANEAN DUCK

1 tablespoon olive oil
4 x 4 oz. boneless duck breasts
2 cooking apples, peeled, cored, and sliced
1¼ cups ready-to-eat prunes
2½ cups dry cider
salt and freshly ground black pepper

Preheat oven to 400F. Heat oil in a shallow flameproof dish, add duck, and cook 3 to 4 minutes on each side, until browned.

1 tablespoon olive oil
4 lb. duck, quartered
1 large onion, thinly sliced
1 clove garlic, crushed
½ teaspoon ground cumin
1¾ cups chicken stock
juice ½ lemon
1 or 2 teaspoons harissa
1 cinnamon stick
1 teaspoon saffron threads
½ cup black olives
½ cup green olives
peel from 1 preserved lemon, rinsed and cut into strips
salt and freshly ground black pepper
2 tablespoons chopped cilantro
cilantro sprigs, to garnish

Cover with apple slices and prunes. Pour cider over duck and season with salt and pepper. Bring to a boil, cover with a lid or piece of aluminum foil, and cook in the oven 55 to 60 minutes, until duck is cooked through. Remove duck from the dish with a slotted spoon, leaving behind apples and prunes, and keep warm.

Heat oil in a flameproof casserole. Add duck and cook until browned all over. Remove with a slotted spoon and set aside. Add onion and garlic to the casserole and cook 5 minutes until soft. Add cumin and cook, stirring, 2 minutes.

Bring cooking juices in the dish to a boil and boil 5 minutes, until liquid has reduced and thickened. Pour sauce, apples, and prunes over duck and serve.

Makes 4 servings.

Add stock, lemon juice, harissa, cinnamon stick, and saffron. Bring to a boil. Return duck to the casserole and add olives and lemon peel. Season with salt and pepper. Simmer gently, partially covered, 45 minutes until duck is cooked through. Discard cinnamon stick. Stir in chopped cilantro, garnish, and serve.

Makes 4 servings.

Note: If preserved lemons are unavailable, use grated zest of 1 fresh lemon instead.

DUCK & OLIVES

3 tablespoons olive oil
4-5 lb. duck, cut into 4 pieces
1 Spanish onion, finely chopped
1 tablespoon plain floor
2 beefsteak tomatoes, peeled (see page 12), seeded, and chopped
¾ cup dry white wine
3 tablespoons water
4 bay leaves
3 sprigs parsley
3 cloves garlic, crushed
salt and freshly ground black pepper
2 cups green olives

Heat half the oil in a heavy flameproof casserole. Add duck in batches, brown evenly, then transfer to absorbent kitchen paper to drain. Heat remaining oil in casserole, add onion, and cook 6 to 8 minutes, stirring occasionally, until golden and translucent. Stir in flour, then tomatoes, wine, water, bay leaves, parsley, and garlic. Season with salt and pepper. Bring to a boil, stirring. Add duck pieces, cover, and cook gently 30 minutes.

Put olives into a bowl, pour over boiling water, then drain well. Add to casserole, cover tightly, and cook about 30 minutes until juices run clear when thickest part of duck is pierced with a skewer. Skim excess fat from surface and adjust seasoning if necessary.

Makes 4 servings.

DUCK & COCONUT CURRY

4 duck portions, skinned
2 tablespoons vegetable oil
1 teaspoon mustard seeds
1 onion, finely chopped
3 cloves garlic, crushed
2 in. piece fresh ginger, grated
2 fresh green chilies, seeded and chopped
1 teaspoon ground cumin
1 tablespoon ground coriander
1 teaspoon turmeric
1 tablespoon white wine vinegar
salt and cayenne pepper
1¼ cups coconut milk
2 tablespoons shredded coconut, toasted, and lemon wedges, to garnish

Wash duck and pat dry with absorbent kitchen paper. Heat oil in a large skillet, add duck, and fry, stirring, over a high heat 8 to 10 minutes, until browned all over, then remove from pan. Pour off all but 2 tablespoons fat from pan, add mustard seeds, and fry 1 minute, or until they begin to pop.

Add onion to pan and cook, stirring, over a medium heat 8 minutes, or until soft and golden. Stir in garlic, ginger, chilies, cumin, coriander, and turmeric and fry 2 minutes. Stir in vinegar and season with salt and cayenne pepper. Return duck to pan and turn pieces to coat them in spice mixture. Stir in coconut milk and bring to a boil. Cover and cook over a low heat about 40 minutes or until duck is tender. Garnish and serve hot.

Makes 4 servings.

PAN-FRIED GAME HENS

1 tablespoon olive oil
2 game hens
4 oz. bacon, chopped
6 oz. button mushrooms
10 shallots
2 tablespoons brandy
1 cup red wine
2½ cups chicken stock
3 tablespoons red currant jelly
salt and freshly ground black pepper
marjoram sprigs, to garnish

Preheat oven to 350F. Heat oil in an ovenproof dish. Add game hens and brown all over.

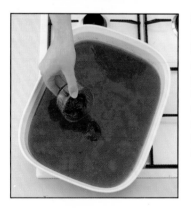

Cover and cook in the oven 35 to 40 minutes. Remove and keep warm. Add bacon, mushrooms, and shallots to the dish and cook, stirring, 4 to 5 minutes, until golden brown. Remove with a slotted spoon and keep warm. Add brandy, wine, stock, and red currant jelly to cooking juices and stir well. Bring to a boil, stirring, and boil 20 to 25 minutes, stirring occasionally, until sauce is reduced and thickened.

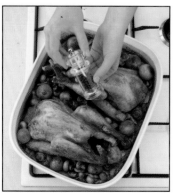

Return game hens, bacon, mushrooms, and shallots to the casserole and season well. Bring to a boil and simmer 4 to 5 minutes to warm through. Cut game hens in half with kitchen scissors or a sharp knife. Garnish with marjoram sprigs and serve.

Makes 4 servings.

GAME HEN FRICASSÉE

2 cloves garlic, crushed
1 teaspoon paprika
1 teaspoon ground ginger
salt and freshly ground black pepper
2 game hens, quartered
2 tablespoons oil
1 large onion, coarsely chopped
8 scallions, sliced
3 tomatoes, peeled (see page 12) and chopped
1 Scotch bonnet chili
1 fresh bay leaf
chicken stock, if required
chopped fresh parsley, to garnish

In a bowl, mix together garlic, paprika, ginger, and seasoning. Rub over game hen portions and place in a dish. Cover and chill overnight. Scrape off and reserve marinade. Pat game hen portions dry with absorbent kitchen paper. Heat oil in a large, heavy skillet and fry game hen pieces, in batches, until golden all over. Transfer to a casserole. Add onion to skillet and cook 10 minutes until soft.

Transfer onion to casserole and add scallions, tomatoes, chili, bay leaf, and reserved marinade. Cover and simmer gently 30 to 40 minutes until game hen is thoroughly cooked. Add a little chicken stock if necessary, although there should not be a large quantity of liquid. Remove and discard chili and bay leaf. Serve garnished with chopped parsley.

Makes 4 servings.

GAME HENS IN BEETS

1 lb. uncooked beets
1 onion, chopped
1¾ cups chicken stock
3 tablespoons butter
1 teaspoon ground cumin
½ teaspoon ground allspice
½ teaspoon ground cinnamon
1 large game hen, quartered
1 teaspoon cornstarch
¼ cup plain yogurt
chopped fresh mint, to garnish

Place beets in a pan of boiling water. Cover and simmer 30 to 60 minutes until tender. Drain.

Preheat the oven to 325F. As soon as beets are cool enough to handle, remove skin. Cut beets into chunks and place in a blender or food processor with onion and chicken stock. Blend until completely smooth. In a flameproof casserole, melt butter. Add cumin, allspice, and cinnamon and cook 1 minute. Add game hen portions and cook until lightly browned.

Stir in beet purée and season with salt and pepper. Heat to simmering point, then cover and cook in the oven 1 hour, or until game hen is very tender. Place game hen portions on a heated serving plate. Blend cornstarch with a little cold water and pour into sauce. Bring to a boil and simmer a minute until slightly thickened. Pour sauce over game hens; drizzle yogurt over, and sprinkle with chopped mint. Serve with rice.

Makes 4 servings.

GAME HEN CASSEROLE

¼ cup olive oil
1 large game hen, quartered
1 large onion, finely sliced
1 clove garlic, crushed
14½ oz. can chopped tomatoes
1 tablespoon chopped fresh oregano
salt and pepper
1 lb. small okra
halved black olives, to garnish

In a flameproof casserole, heat oil. Add game hen pieces. Cook on both sides until brown. Transfer to a plate.

Add onion and garlic to casserole and cook until soft. Add tomatoes, oregano, 1¼ cups water, salt, and pepper. Bring to a boil, then add game hen and coat well with sauce. Cover pan and simmer gently 40 minutes.

Trim ends of okra without cutting pods. Put into a bowl of cold water, rinse gently, and strain. Repeat until water is clear. Spread okra over game hens. Cover and simmer an additional 30 minutes until okra is tender. Sprinkle the top with black olives and serve.

Makes 4 servings.

SPANISH PARTRIDGE

2 partridges, halved along backbone
2 tablespoons brandy
salt and freshly ground black pepper
3 tablespoons olive oil
1 Spanish onion, chopped
3 cloves garlic, finely chopped
2 tablespoons all-purpose flour
¼ cup red wine vinegar
1 cup red wine
1 cup chicken stock
6 black peppercorns
2 cloves
1 bay leaf
2 carrots, cut into short lengths
8 shallots
¼ cup grated unsweetened chocolate

Rub partridges with brandy, salt, and pepper
and set aside 30 minutes. Heat oil in a heavy
flameproof casserole into which the birds fit
snugly. Add onion and fry, stirring
occasionally, 3 minutes. Stir in garlic and
cook 2 minutes.

Sprinkle birds lightly with flour, then fry in
casserole 5 minutes on each side. Remove
and set aside.

Stir vinegar into casserole and boil 1 to 2
minutes. Add wine and boil 1 to 2 minutes,
then add stock, peppercorns, cloves, bay leaf,
and partridges. Heat to simmering point,
cover tightly, and cook gently 40 minutes.
Add carrots and shallots, cover again, and
continue to cook gently 20 minutes.

Transfer partridges, shallots, and carrots to a
warm dish. If necessary boil cooking juices
until reduced to 1¼ cups, then purée in a
blender or food processor.

Return juices to casserole, heat gently, and stir
in grated chocolate until melted. Return
partridges and vegetables to casserole and
turn them over in sauce so they are well
coated.

Makes 4 servings.

PHEASANT IN PARSLEY SAUCE

½ stick butter
2 pheasants
3 oz. fresh parsley
3 onions, thinly sliced
¼ cup all-purpose flour
1¼ cups chicken stock
⅔ cup thick sour cream
salt and freshly ground black pepper
Italian parsley sprigs, to garnish

Preheat oven to 350F. Melt butter in a large flameproof dish. Add pheasants and cook until browned all over. Remove and keep warm.

Separate thick parsley stalks from the leaves and tie stalks together with string. Chop leaves and set aside. Add onions to the dish and cook, stirring occasionally, 7 minutes, until soft and lightly colored. Add flour and cook, stirring, 1 minute. Gradually add chicken stock, stirring constantly until smooth. Bring to a boil and add bundle of parsley stalks. Add pheasants, cover, and cook in the oven 1 hour.

Remove pheasants from the dish and keep warm. Remove and discard parsley stalks. Add chopped parsley and thick sour cream to sauce and season with salt and pepper. Heat gently to warm through. Cut pheasants in half with kitchen scissors. Garnish with Italian parsley sprigs and serve with parsley sauce.

Makes 4 servings.

SQUAB STIFADO

4 squabs
2 tablespoons seasoned flour
⅓ cup olive oil
1 lb. tiny pickling onions, peeled
1 clove garlic, crushed
1 tablespoon tomato paste
¾ cup red wine
1 cup chicken stock
1 fresh bay leaf
2 sprigs thyme
salt and freshly ground black pepper
2 slices white bread, crusts removed
2 tablespoons chopped fresh parsley

Toss squabs in seasoned flour.

Preheat the oven to 325F. Heat half the oil in a flameproof casserole. Add squabs and cook until browned all over. Remove and set aside. Add onions to the casserole and cook 7 minutes until beginning to brown. Add garlic and tomato paste and stir in wine and stock. Add bay leaf, thyme, and salt and pepper. Return squabs to the casserole, cover, and cook in the oven 1½ to 2 hours until squabs are cooked through and tender. Transfer squabs to a warmed serving dish and keep warm.

Remove herbs from cooking liquid and, if desired, reduce cooking liquid by boiling over a high heat 1 to 2 minutes. Cut each slice of bread into four triangles. Heat remaining oil in a skillet, add bread, and fry until golden brown on both sides. Dip one edge of each triangle into parsley. Pour sauce over squabs, garnish with fried bread, and serve.

Makes 4 servings.

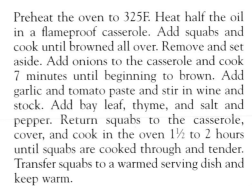

QUAIL WITH FIGS & ORANGES

3 tablespoon olive oil
8 quails
1 onion, thinly sliced
2 stalks celery, thinly sliced
⅔ cup dry white wine
⅔ cup hot chicken stock
salt and freshly ground black pepper
2 oranges
4 figs

Preheat oven to 325F. Heat 2 tablespoons of the olive oil in a heavy casserole. Add quails and cook until browned all over. Remove and set aside.

Add onion and celery to the casserole and cook gently 7 minutes until soft and lightly browned. Replace quails and pour over wine and hot stock. Season with salt and pepper. Cover and cook in the oven 30 to 40 minutes until quails are cooked through. Just before the end of the cooking time, preheat the broiler. Peel oranges, removing all the pith and cut each one into four thick slices. Cut figs in half.

Brush orange slices with olive oil and broil 2 to 3 minutes. Turn, add figs, and broil cut sides 2 minutes. Set aside and keep warm. Transfer quails, onion, and celery to a warmed serving dish. Pour over cooking juices, arrange oranges and figs around the birds, and serve.

Makes 4 servings.

QUAIL IN RUM & RAISIN SAUCE

¼ cup dark rum
¼ cup raisins
1 tablespoon oil
8 quails
1 onion, sliced
1 clove garlic, sliced
1 teaspoon molasses
⅔ cup chicken stock
1 teaspoon hot pepper sauce
salt and freshly ground black pepper
2 teaspoons arrowroot
chopped cilantro, to garnish

Put rum and raisins in a bowl and let soak 2 hours.

Heat oil in a flameproof casserole. Add quails and cook, turning frequently, until evenly browned. Remove and set aside. Add onion and garlic to casserole and cook 10 minutes until soft. Strain rum from raisins and put in a ladle or small saucepan. Heat gently, then set alight with a taper and pour into casserole.

When flames die down, stir in molasses, stock, hot pepper sauce, and seasoning. Return quails to casserole. Cover and cook 20 to 30 minutes until cooked through. Remove to a serving dish and keep warm. In a bowl, mix arrowroot with a little water and stir into sauce in casserole. Cook, stirring, a few minutes until thickened, then pour over quails. Garnish with chopped cilantro and serve.

Makes 4 servings.

PROVENÇAL RABBIT

3 oz. pancetta
2 tablespoons olive oil
1 onion, chopped
4 rabbit portions
1 tablespoon seasoned flour
3 tablespoons tapénade
1¾ cups chicken stock
⅔ cup dry white wine
2 fresh bay leaves
2 sprigs thyme
salt and freshly ground black pepper
1 small fennel bulb, roughly chopped
black olives and fennel leaves, to garnish

Roughly chop half the pancetta.

Preheat the oven to 350F. Heat half the oil in a flameproof casserole. Add onion and chopped pancetta and cook 3 minutes. Remove with a slotted spoon and set aside. Dust rabbit portions with seasoned flour. Heat remaining oil in the casserole, add rabbit, and cook until browned all over. Mix together tapénade, stock, and wine and pour over rabbit. Add onion, pancetta, bay leaves, and thyme. Season with salt and pepper and bring to a boil. Cover and cook in the oven 45 minutes.

Add fennel and cook 45 minutes, or until rabbit is cooked through and tender. Broil remaining pancetta until crisp, then snip into small pieces and sprinkle over rabbit. Garnish with olives and fennel leaves and serve.

Makes 4 servings.

RABBIT IN MUSTARD SAUCE

½ stick butter
8 rabbit portions
1 cup dry white wine
½ cup Dijon-style mustard
1 thyme sprig
salt and freshly ground black pepper
½ cup plain yogurt
chopped fresh Italian parsley and thyme sprigs, to garnish

Melt butter in a flameproof casserole. Add rabbit and cook 5 to 10 minutes, turning, until browned all over. Remove with a slotted spoon.

Stir in wine, mustard, thyme, and salt and pepper and bring to a boil. Return rabbit to the casserole, cover, and simmer 25 minutes. Remove rabbit with a slotted spoon and keep warm.

Boil sauce until reduced by half. Remove and discard thyme sprig and stir in yogurt. Heat gently to warm through. Garnish rabbit with chopped parsley and thyme sprigs, pour over sauce, and serve.

Makes 4 servings.

RABBIT & RED BELL PEPPER STEW

2¼ lb. rabbit pieces
2 tablespoons chopped fresh thyme
2 tablespoons chopped fresh rosemary
2 fresh bay leaves
juice 1 lemon
1 tablespoon balsamic vinegar
salt and freshly ground black pepper
2 tablespoons olive oil
4 red bell peppers, seeded and roughly diced
14½ oz. can strained crushed tomatoes

Place rabbit in a plastic bag with thyme, rosemary, bay leaves, lemon juice, vinegar, salt, and pepper. Seal and let marinate in the refrigerator 2 to 3 hours or overnight.

Heat half the oil in a saucepan. Add bell peppers and cook over gentle heat about 10 minutes until soft. Stir in tomatoes and season with salt and pepper. Cover and cook 30 minutes. Remove rabbit from marinade, reserving marinade, and pat dry with absorbent kitchen paper.

Heat remaining oil in a skillet, add rabbit pieces, and fry on all sides until golden. Add rabbit to bell pepper sauce. Deglaze skillet with reserved marinade and add to rabbit. Cover and simmer 20 to 30 minutes until rabbit is tender. Serve with pasta.

Makes 4 servings.

CALYPSO RABBIT

juice 1 lime
salt and freshly ground black pepper
½ teaspoon chopped fresh thyme
2 cloves garlic, crushed
6 boneless rabbit portions
3 tablespoons oil
2 teaspoons brown sugar
¼ cup cashews
2 large onions, chopped
4 oz. mushrooms, sliced
1 in. piece fresh ginger, grated
¼ cup chicken stock
few drops Angostura bitters
2 teaspoons arrowroot
thyme sprigs and lime slices, to garnish

In a dish, mix together lime juice, seasoning, thyme, and 1 garlic clove. Add rabbit pieces and turn in marinade to coat thoroughly. Cover and leave in a cool place 3 hours. In a flameproof casserole, heat half the oil. Add sugar and cook gently until bubbling. Add rabbit and fry, turning until evenly browned. Meanwhile, in a skillet, heat remaining oil. Add cashews and cook gently until lightly browned. Remove with a slotted spoon and set aside.

Add onions to pan and cook 5 minutes. Stir in remaining garlic, mushrooms, and ginger and cook 5 minutes. Stir in stock and Angostura bitters and pour over rabbit. Stir in half the cashews. Cover casserole and simmer gently 30 to 40 minutes until rabbit is cooked through. In a bowl, mix arrowroot with a little water. Stir into rabbit mixture and simmer 3 minutes. Sprinkle with remaining cashews and garnish with thyme and lime slices. Serve with rice.

Makes 6 servings.

BEEF & VEAL

BELGIAN HOTCHPOTCH

8 oz. brisket of beef, diced
8 oz. shoulder of lamb, diced
3 oz. side of pork, diced
2¼ cups chicken stock
2 bay leaves
4 oz. rutabaga, diced
10 small onions
8 oz. Brussels sprouts
1½ lb. potatoes, diced
1 carrot, diced
8 oz. pork chipolata sausages
⅔ cup thick sour cream

Put beef, lamb, and pork in a flameproof casserole and pour in stock.

Add 2¼ cups water, bay leaves, and 1 teaspoon salt. Bring to a boil, skimming any scum from the surface. Cover tightly and simmer 2 hours. Add rutabaga, onions, Brussels sprouts, potatoes, and carrots and cook 30 minutes, until meat is tender. Remove meat and vegetables from the casserole with a slotted spoon and keep warm. Put sausages in the casserole and cook 10 minutes. Remove with a slotted spoon and add to meat and vegetables.

Bring sauce to a boil and boil until reduced by one-third. Season with salt and pepper, stir in thick sour cream, and heat gently to warm through. Pour sauce over meat and vegetables and serve.

Makes 4 to 6 servings.

POT ROAST OF BRISKET

3 lb. brisket of beef
2 leeks, thickly sliced
1 bay leaf
2 parsley stalks
1 celery leaf
5 medium carrots, thickly sliced
1 lb. sweet potatoes, cut into chunks
¼ cup cider vinegar
½ small white cabbage, thickly shredded
salt and freshly ground black pepper

Heat a large flameproof casserole, add brisket, and cook, turning, 3 to 4 minutes, until browned all over.

Remove from the casserole. Add leeks and mix into cooking juices. With a piece of string, tie together bay leaf, parsley stalks ,and celery leaf and add to the casserole with carrots and sweet potatoes. Stir well. Add vinegar and ½ cup water. Put meat on top.

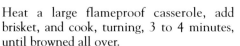

Cover and cook very gently 2½ hours. Remove beef from the casserole and keep warm. Remove vegetables with a slotted spoon and keep warm. Bring sauce to a boil and add white cabbage. Season and simmer 5 minutes. Carve beef and serve with vegetables.

Makes 6 to 8 servings.

BOEUF EN DAUBE PROVENÇAL

2¼ lb. braising steak, diced
1 Spanish onion, chopped
3 cloves garlic, chopped
bouquet garni
3 cups full-bodied red wine
1 teaspoon black peppercorns
2 tablespoons olive oil
8 oz. bacon, cut into strips
3 tomatoes, peeled, seeded, and chopped
2 in. wide strip of orange peel, oven-dried
12 black olives
Italian parsley sprigs, to garnish

Put steak, onion, garlic, bouquet garni, wine, and peppercorns in a non-metallic bowl.

Cover and let marinate 12 to 24 hours. Preheat oven to 325F. Remove meat from marinade with a slotted spoon, reserving marinade, and drain beef on absorbent kitchen paper. Heat oil in a heavy flameproof casserole, add bacon, and cook until browned. Remove with a slotted spoon and set aside. Add beef and cook over a moderately high heat until browned all over. Add tomatoes and cook 2 to 3 minutes.

Add reserved marinade, bacon, and orange peel and season with salt and pepper. Heat to almost simmering, cover tightly, and cook in oven 3¼ hours. Add olives and cook 15 minutes. Discard bouquet garni and orange peel, garnish with parsley, and serve.

Makes 4 to 6 servings.

Note: To dry orange peel, put in a very low oven and leave until hard.

BOEUF BOURGUIGNON

1 or 2 tablespoons olive oil
2 slices thick-cut bacon, chopped
12 each button onions and button mushrooms
2¼ lb. braising steak, diced
1 large onion, finely chopped
1 carrot, finely chopped
3 cloves garlic, chopped
1 tablespoon all-purpose flour
3 cups red Burgundy wine
bouquet garni
salt and freshly ground black pepper
fresh parsley and bay leaves, to garnish

Heat 1 tablespoon oil in a heavy flameproof casserole and cook bacon 2 to 3 minutes.

Remove with a slotted spoon and set aside. Add button onions to casserole and cook, stirring occasionally, until browned. Remove with a slotted spoon and set aside. Add mushrooms to casserole and cook, stirring occasionally, until lightly browned, adding more oil if necessary. Remove with a slotted spoon and set aside. Add beef to casserole and cook over a moderately high heat until browned all over. Remove with a slotted spoon and set aside.

Add chopped onion and carrot to casserole and cook, stirring occasionally, until beginning to brown. Return bacon and beef to casserole, add garlic, and stir in flour. Stir in wine, bouquet garni, salt, and plenty of pepper. Heat to almost simmering, cover, and cook very gently 2¾ hours, stirring occasionally. Add reserved onions and mushrooms, cover and cook 10 minutes, to warm through. Garnish with parsley and bay leaves and serve.

Makes 4 servings.

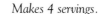

BEEF IN CHILI SAUCE

DRY BEEF WITH COCONUT

8 dried red chilies, cored, seeded and chopped
2 small onions, chopped
2 in. piece fresh ginger, chopped
1½ lb. lean beef, cut into bite-size pieces
1 tablespoon ground coriander
1 tablespoon ground cumin
1 tablespoon tomato ketchup
2 teaspoons turmeric
2 teaspoons paprika
2 tablespoons vegetable oil
2 cloves garlic, crushed
1 in. stick cinnamon
seeds from 3 cardamom pods, crushed
½ star anise
sugar and salt
1 onion, sliced into thick rings

¼ cup vegetable oil
6 shallots, finely chopped
3 cloves garlic, finely chopped
1 fresh red chili, cored, seeded and finely chopped
1½ lb. lean beef, thinly sliced and cut into ½ in.
   strips
1 tablespoon light brown sugar
1½ teaspoons ground cumin
1 teaspoon ground coriander
squeeze of lime juice
salt
½ fresh coconut, shredded, or 2⅔ cups dried
   coconut

Put chilies in a small blender. Add ¼ **cup** hot water and leave until slightly softened. Add half of small onions and half of ginger to blender and mix to a paste. Put beef in a large bowl. Add spice paste from blender, coriander, cumin, tomato ketchup, turmeric, and paprika. Stir together. Cover and leave at least 1 hour to marinate.

In a wok or sauté pan, heat 1 tablespoon oil over medium heat. Add shallots, garlic, and chili and fry about 5 minutes, stirring occasionally, until softened but not browned. Add beef, sugar, cumin, coriander, lime juice, salt to taste, and ⅔ cup water. Cover pan tightly and simmer gently 30 minutes, stirring occasionally.

Heat oil in a wok, add remaining onion and ginger, and garlic. Fry, stirring, 3 minutes until lightly browned. Stir in cinnamon stick, cardamom, and star anise and cook 1 minute. Add meat and marinade and cook over medium-high heat, stirring, 5 minutes. Add 1½ cups water and sugar and salt to taste. Cover pan. Simmer very gently 1¼ hours or until beef is tender, stirring occasionally. Add onion rings and cook 3 to 5 minutes or until soft.

Makes 4 to 6 servings.

Uncover pan and stir in coconut until all liquid has been absorbed. Stir in remaining oil and continue stirring until coconut begins to brown.

Makes 6 servings.

CURRIED COCONUT BEEF

6¾ cups coconut milk
4 fresh bay leaves
3 lb. braising steak, cut into 2 in. cubes
CURRY PASTE
6 shallots, chopped
6 cloves garlic, smashed
6 fresh red chilies, cored, seeded and chopped
3 in. piece galangal, chopped
2 stalks lemon grass, chopped
1 in. piece cinnamon stick
12 whole cloves
1 teaspoon ground turmeric

Mix all curry paste ingredients in a blender. Add a little coconut milk, if necessary.

In a saucepan, combine curry paste and coconut milk. Add bay leaves and bring to a boil over high heat, stirring occasionally. Lower heat to medium and cook sauce, stirring occasionally, 15 minutes.

Stir in beef. Simmer, uncovered, stirring occasionally, 2 hours. Reduce heat to very low and cook beef an additional 1½ to 2 hours until sauce is quite thick. Stir frequently to prevent sticking. Skim fat and oil from surface. Serve with boiled rice.

Makes 8 servings.

GARLIC BEEF CASSEROLE

1 tablespoon peanut oil
1 lb. lean beef chuck, trimmed and cut into ¾ in. cubes
2 shallots, chopped
4 cloves garlic, thinly sliced
2 large carrots, sliced
6 oz. baby corn, halved lengthwise
8 oz. button mushrooms
1¼ cups beef stock
2 tablespoons dark soy sauce
1 tablespoon rice wine
2 teaspoons five-spice powder
2 tablespoons hoisin sauce
1 teaspoon chili sauce

Heat oil in a nonstick or well-seasoned wok and stir-fry beef, shallots, garlic, carrots, baby corn and mushrooms 5 minutes. Add stock, soy sauce, rice wine, five-spice powder, hoisin sauce, and chili sauce and bring to a boil. Reduce to a simmer, cover, and simmer 1 hour.

Remove from heat and blot surface with absorbent kitchen paper to absorb surface fat. Increase the heat and boil 10 minutes to reduce and thicken sauce. Serve with rice.

Makes 4 servings.

BEEF IN BAROLO WINE

2¼ lb. braising beef joint
6 cloves garlic, crushed
1 onion, roughly chopped
1 carrot, chopped
1 stalk celery, chopped
2 bay leaves
2 large thyme sprigs
2 or 3 peppercorns, lightly crushed
2 cloves
2 allspice berries, crushed
½ cup Barolo wine, or other full-bodied red wine
2 tablespoons olive oil
2 tablespoons tomato paste
⅔ cup strong beef stock
salt and freshly ground black pepper

Place meat in a plastic bag with garlic, onion, carrot, celery, bay leaves, thyme, peppercorns, cloves, allspice, and wine. Shake the bag, seal, and refrigerate several hours or overnight, turning meat occasionally. Next day, preheat oven to 325F. Open bag, remove meat from marinade, and pat dry with absorbent kitchen paper. Heat oil in a large flameproof casserole and brown meat all over. Pour in reserved marinade, tomato paste, and stock. Cover tightly and bake in oven 2 to 3 hours until beef is tender.

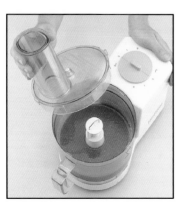

Lift meat out of casserole and keep warm. Skim off any fat, remove bay leaves from sauce. Purée sauce in a blender or food processor until smooth. Taste and season. The sauce should be quite thick; if it is not, boil to reduce it. Slice meat thinly and serve with sauce.

Makes 8 servings.

CARBONNADE DE BOEUF

2 tablespoons olive oil
2¼ lb. braising steak, diced
3 or 4 medium onions, sliced
2 tablespoons all-purpose flour
2½ cups brown ale
1 clove garlic, crushed
bouquet garni
4 thick slices French bread
salt and freshly ground black pepper
Dijon-style mustard, for spreading
Italian parsley and chopped fresh parsley, to garnish

Heat oil in a heavy flameproof casserole, add meat, and cook until browned all over. Remove with a slotted spoon and set aside.

Add onions to casserole and cook gently, stirring occasionally, 10 minutes, until browned. Sprinkle in flour and cook, stirring, until lightly browned. Stir in beer and bring to a boil, stirring. Return beef to casserole, add garlic and bouquet garni, cover tightly, and cook very gently 2 hours, stirring occasionally.

Preheat broiler to low. Toast bread slowly until crisp and golden. Spread thickly with mustard, baste lightly with sauce from casserole, and toast 5 to 10 minutes, until topping is browned. Garnish casserole with parsley and serve with mustard croûtes.

Makes 4 servings.

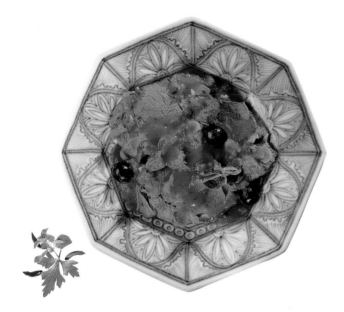

BEEF WITH TOMATO SAUCE

2 cloves garlic, thinly sliced
1 tablespoon finely chopped fresh thyme
1 tablespoon finely chopped fresh marjoram
1½ lb. piece chuck steak
2 tablespoons olive oil
SAUCE:
2 tablespoons olive oil
8 cloves garlic, chopped
1 sprig thyme
2 sprigs marjoram
3 sprigs parsley
14½ oz. can chopped tomatoes
8 canned anchovy fillets, chopped
¾ cup dry white wine
24 small pitted black olives
salt and freshly ground black pepper

To make sauce, heat oil in a saucepan, add garlic, thyme, marjoram, and parsley and cook gently 5 minutes. Add tomatoes with their juice, then stir in anchovies, wine, and olives. Simmer 15 minutes. Taste and adjust seasoning.

Meanwhile, mix sliced garlic with chopped thyme and marjoram. Using the point of a sharp knife, cut small slits in beef and push herb-covered slices of garlic deep into slits. Heat oil in a flameproof casserole, add beef, and cook until evenly browned, 10 minutes. Pour over sauce, cover tightly, and cook gently about 1½ hours turning beef occasionally, until it is tender.

Makes 4 servings.

BEEF IN SPINACH SAUCE

2 tablespoons olive oil
1½ lb. chuck steak, cut into 1½ in. cubes
8 button onions
1 tablespoon red wine vinegar
8 oz. fresh spinach, trimmed
1 tablespoon breadcrumbs
3 cloves garlic
2 cups veal stock or water
salt and freshly ground black pepper
1 tablespoon black olive paste

In a large, flameproof casserole, heat oil, add beef, and brown on all sides. Remove and set aside. Add onions to casserole and cook, stirring frequently, until evenly browned. Stir in vinegar and boil 1 minute.

Put spinach, breadcrumbs, garlic, and half the stock or water in a blender or food processor and mix until smooth. Return beef to casserole, pour over spinach mixture with remaining stock or water. Season. Heat to simmering point, then cover, and simmer very gently 1½ to 2 hours until beef is tender. Stir in black olive paste and serve.

Makes 4 to 6 servings.

CHILI BEEF WITH NACHOS

1 tablespoon olive oil
1 onion, chopped
1 clove garlic, crushed
1 lb. ground beef
15 oz. can red kidney beans, drained
1 green bell pepper, chopped
2 tablespoons tomato paste
2 teaspoons chili powder
5 oz. tortilla chips
1 cup shredded mozzarella cheese
1 or 2 teaspoons paprika

Heat oil in a flameproof casserole. Add onion and garlic and cook, stirring occasionally, 5 minutes, until soft. Add ground beef and cook 6 to 8 minutes, until brown. Stir in kidney beans, bell pepper, tomato paste, chili powder, and ⅔ cup water. Cover and simmer 10 to 15 minutes. Preheat oven to 400F.

Uncover and cook 5 minutes, until sauce is reduced and thickened. Arrange tortilla chips over the top, sprinkle with mozzarella cheese and paprika, and cook in the oven 20 minutes until cheese is melted and golden. Serve.

Makes 4 servings.

BEEF TAGINE WITH PRUNES

1¼ cups pitted prunes
1 teaspoon ground ginger
1 tablespoon ground coriander
pinch saffron threads
salt and freshly ground black pepper
3 tablespoons olive oil
2½ lb. stewing beef, diced
2 onions, sliced
2 cloves garlic, crushed
chicken stock or water
1 cinnamon stick
1 tablespoon clear honey
1 teaspoon harissa
1 tablespoon sesame seeds
3 tablespoons chopped fresh parsley
1 teaspoon orange flower water, to serve

Place prunes in a bowl and cover with boiling water. Let soak 2 hours. In a large bowl, mix together ginger, coriander, saffron, salt, bell pepper, and 2 tablespoons of oil. Add beef and mix well, rubbing the spices into the meat with your fingers. Transfer to a tagine or casserole. In a large skillet, heat remaining oil. Add onions and garlic and cook 10 minutes until soft. Add to spiced beef, then pour in enough stock or water to barely cover meat. Add cinnamon.

Cover the tagine and simmer gently 2 hours until beef is tender. Check from time to time and add more liquid, if necessary. Drain prunes and add to the casserole; simmer 20 minutes longer. Stir in honey and harissa and cook an additional 15 minutes. Dry-fry sesame seeds in a skillet until lightly browned. To serve, stir in parsley, sprinkle with orange flower water and sesame seeds. Serve with couscous.

Makes 6 servings.

JAMAICAN BELL PEPPERPOT

2 tablespoons oil
2 onions, chopped
2 cloves garlic, crushed
1¼ lb. fore shank of beef, diced
2½ cups beef stock
1 lb. fresh spinach
1 teaspoon dried thyme
2 fresh green chilies, seeded and chopped
1 or 2 sweet potatoes
2 cups diced pumpkin
1 green bell pepper, chopped
2 tomatoes, peeled (see page 12) and chopped
salt and 2 teaspoons hot pepper sauce
2 cups all-purpose flour
1 tablespoon baking powder
2 tablespoons butter

In a flameproof casserole, heat oil. Add onions and garlic and cook 10 minutes until soft. Remove and set aside. Add beef to hot oil and fry in batches, until browned. Return onions and browned meat to casserole. Add stock, cover, and simmer gently 1½ hours. Cook spinach in a little water then drain thoroughly and process in a food processor. Add to casserole with thyme, chilies, sweet potato, pumpkin, bell pepper, tomatoes, salt and hot pepper sauce. Cook an additional 30 minutes until beef and vegetables are tender.

Meanwhile, make dumplings: sift flour, baking powder, and a little salt into a bowl. Rub in butter and add enough cold water to make a dough. Shape into balls about 1½ in. in diameter and flatten slightly. Drop into very gently simmering casserole about 10 minutes before end of cooking time.

Makes 4 to 6 servings.

MADRAS MEAT CURRY

1½ lb. braising steak
2 tablespoons vegetable oil
1 large onion, finely sliced
4 cloves
4 green cardamom pods, bruised
3 fresh green chilies, seeded and finely chopped
2 dry red chilies, seeded and crushed
1 in. piece fresh ginger, grated
2 cloves garlic, crushed
2 teaspoons ground coriander
2 teaspoons turmeric
¼ cup tamarind juice, see Note
salt
lettuce leaves, to garnish

Cut beef into 1 in. cubes. Heat oil in a large heavy-bottomed pan, add beef, and fry until browned all over. Remove with a slotted spoon and set aside. Add onion, cloves, and cardamom pods to pan and fry about 8 minutes, stirring, until onion is soft and golden brown. Stir in chilies, ginger, garlic, coriander, and turmeric and fry 2 minutes. Return beef to pan, add ¼ cup water, and simmer, covered, 1 hour.

Stir in tamarind juice and season with salt, re-cover and simmer, covered, 15 to 30 minutes, until beef is tender. Serve garnished with lettuce leaves.

Makes 4 servings.

Note: Tamarind pulp, available in Indian shops, is used to make tamarind juice. Soak a walnut-sized piece in 1 cup boiling water 20 minutes, then squeeze pulp in cheesecloth to extract juice. Discard pulp.

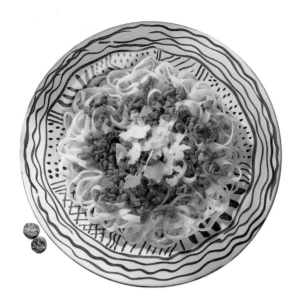

PASTA BOLOGNESE

3 oz. pancetta or bacon in a piece, diced
1 medium onion, finely chopped
1 medium carrot, finely diced
1 stalk celery, finely chopped
8 oz. lean ground beef
4 oz. chicken livers, trimmed and chopped
1 medium potato, shredded
2 tablespoons tomato paste
½ cup white wine
1 cup beef stock or water
salt and freshly ground black pepper
freshly grated nutmeg
14 oz. dried spaghetti, fettuccine or tagliatelle
freshly grated Parmesan cheese, to serve (optional)

Heat a saucepan and add pancetta. Cook in its own fat 2 to 3 minutes until browning. Add onion, carrot, and celery and brown. Stir in ground beef and brown over high heat, breaking it up with a wooden spoon. Stir in chicken livers and cook 2 to 3 minutes.

Add shredded potato and tomato paste, mix well, and pour in wine and stock. Season with salt, pepper, and nutmeg. Bring to a boil, half-cover, and simmer 35 minutes until reduced and thickened, stirring occasionally. Meanwhile, cook pasta in boiling salted water until tender. Drain well and toss with sauce. Serve with Parmesan cheese, if desired.

Makes 6 servings.

BEEF GOULASH WITH CHILI

2 tablespoons olive oil
1 onion, sliced
1 clove garlic, crushed
2 teaspoons paprika
1½ lb. lean stewing beef, diced
pinch caraway seeds
2 bay leaves
1 tablespoon balsamic vinegar
2 cups beef stock
salt and freshly ground black pepper
1½ lb. potatoes, diced
2 green bell peppers, sliced
1 fresh green chili, cored, seeded and sliced
14½ oz. can chopped tomatoes
2 tablespoons tomato paste

Heat oil in a flameproof casserole. Add onion, garlic, and paprika and cook, stirring, 2 minutes. Add beef and cook 3 to 4 minutes, until onion is soft and beef has browned. Add caraway seeds, bay leaves, vinegar, and half the stock. Season with salt and pepper and bring to a boil. Cover and simmer 1 hour.

Stir in remaining stock, potatoes, bell peppers, chili, tomatoes, and tomato paste. Bring to a boil, cover, and simmer 30 to 40 minutes, until meat and vegetables are tender.

Makes 4 servings.

SPICY BRAISED BEEF

GARLIC BEEF

3 lb. beef round joint
2 cloves garlic, crushed
½ teaspoon ground cinnamon
¼ teaspoon ground cloves
salt and pepper
3 tablespoons olive oil
4 onions, thinly sliced
½ cup red wine
2 tablespoons tomato paste
1 lb. spaghetti
1 tablespoon balsamic vinegar
fresh herbs, to garnish

With a sharp knife, make slits in beef.

2 tablespoons olive oil
4 oz. piece unsmoked bacon, cut into 2 in. cubes
2¼ lb. chuck steak, cut into 1½ in. cubes
1 Spanish onion, chopped
1 head garlic, divided into cloves
1 cup red wine
2 cloves
bouquet garni of 1 sprig marjoram, 1 sprig thyme,
   2 sprigs parsley and 1 bay leaf
salt and freshly ground black pepper

In a bowl, mix garlic, cinnamon, cloves, salt, and pepper. Press mixture into slits and leave beef in a cool place 1 hour. Heat oil in a flameproof casserole into which meat will just fit. Turn meat in hot oil until brown all over. Remove from casserole. Add onions and cook gently until soft and lightly browned. Replace meat. Add wine and enough hot water to barely cover it. Mix tomato paste with a little water; stir into casserole, and season.

In a heavy flameproof casserole, heat oil, add bacon, and cook over a low heat until bacon gives off its fat. Increase heat, add beef, and cook about 5 minutes, stirring occasionally, until browned all over. Using a slotted spoon, transfer beef and bacon to a bowl.

Cover casserole and cook over a gentle heat about 1½ hours, turning meat frequently, until it is tender. Bring a large pan of salted water to a boil and cook spaghetti until *al dente*. Remove meat and keep hot. Add vinegar to sauce. Boil briskly until reduced to a smooth glossy sauce. Slice beef. Garnish with herbs and serve with some sauce poured over beef and remainder stirred into spaghetti.

Makes 6 servings.

Stir onion and garlic into casserole and cook gently 6 minutes, stirring occasionally. Stir in wine, cloves, bouquet garni, and salt and pepper. Return meat to casserole, cover tightly, and cook gently 2 hours, stirring occasionally, until meat is very tender. Check from time to time to ensure casserole is not drying out.

Makes 6 servings.

VEAL WITH MUSHROOMS

2 tablespoons olive oil
6 slices bacon, cut into thin strips
4 x 8 oz. slices veal shank
3 or 4 carrots, cut into thick strips
4 plum tomatoes, peeled, quartered and seeded
2½ cups beef stock
½ cup red wine
1 lb. mixed mushrooms
½ stick) butter, diced
1½ cups chopped fresh parsley

Heat oil in a flameproof casserole. Add bacon and cook 3 to 4 minutes. Remove and drain on absorbent kitchen paper. Add veal and cook until browned on both sides.

Remove veal and drain on absorbent kitchen paper. Add carrots and tomatoes to the casserole and cook 2 to 3 minutes. Return veal to the casserole. Pour over stock and red wine. Bring to a boil, cover, and simmer 40 minutes. Add mushrooms and bacon and cook 10 minutes, until veal is cooked through and tender.

Lift out veal and remove carrots, mushrooms, and bacon with a slotted spoon. Keep warm. Strain sauce and return to the casserole. Bring to a boil and boil until reduced by one-third. Whisk in butter, a little at a time. Stir in parsley. Return bacon and vegetables to sauce and cook gently 2 minutes, to warm through. Arrange veal on warmed serving plates, pour sauce over, and serve.

Makes 4 servings.

SOFRITO

¼ cup olive oil
1 onion, finely chopped
1 clove garlic, crushed
1½ lb. thin veal slices
seasoned flour
2 tablespoons brandy
⅔ cup white wine
1¼ cups beef stock
salt and pepper
3 tablespoons chopped fresh parsley
parsley, to garnish

In a skillet, heat oil. Add onion and garlic; cook until soft. Transfer to a flame-proof casserole.

Coat meat lightly with seasoned flour. Fry in skillet until brown on both sides. Add brandy. When brandy has stopped bubbling, transfer meat to casserole.

Add wine, stock, salt, and pepper. Cover and cook gently 45 minutes until meat is tender and sauce lightly thickened. Stir in parsley. Garnish with more parsley.

Makes 6 servings.

LAMB

LAMB CHOP BOULANGERE

1 tablespoon olive oil
4 x 6 oz. lamb loin chops
2 large onions, sliced
8 oz. Savoy cabbage, shredded
1 lb. old potatoes, thinly sliced
salt and freshly ground black pepper
fresh bouquet garni
2¼ cups lamb or chicken stock
2 tablespoons butter, melted
chopped fresh parsley, to garnish

Heat oil in a flameproof casserole. Add chops, and cook 2 to 3 minutes on each side until browned. Remove and set aside.

Preheat oven to 400F. Add onions and cabbage to the casserole and cook gently 10 minutes, until soft. Remove half the mixture and set aside. Place chops on top of remaining onion and cabbage mixture. Mix two-thirds of the potatoes with reserved onion and cabbage mixture. Season with salt and pepper. Arrange on top of chops, placing bouquet garni in the middle. Pour over stock.

Arrange remaining potatoes on top and brush with melted butter. Cook in the oven 15 minutes. Remove from the oven and press potatoes down. Brush again with melted butter and season with salt and pepper. Lower oven temperature to 350F and cook 1 hour. Garnish with chopped parsley and serve.

Makes 4 servings.

SAGE LAMB COBBLER

2 lb. neck of lamb, boned and diced
¼ cup all-purpose flour
1 tablespoon olive oil
1 large onion, chopped
¼ cup dried peas, soaked overnight
2 or 3 carrots
1¼ cups diced rutabaga
2¼ cups lamb or chicken stock
salt, pepper and large pinch paprika
TOPPING:
2 cups all-purpose flour
1½ teaspoons baking powder
½ stick butter
1 teaspoon dried sage
1 egg
2 tablespoons milk, plus extra for brushing

Preheat oven to 325F. Coat lamb in flour. Heat oil in a flameproof casserole. Add lamb and cook until browned all over. Remove and set aside. Add onion and cook, stirring occasionally, 7 minutes, until lightly browned. Return lamb and add peas, carrots, and rutabaga. Pour in stock and season with salt, pepper, and paprika. Bring to a boil, cover, and cook in the oven 2 hours.

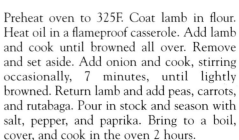

Sift flour, baking powder, and salt into a bowl. Rub in butter until mixture resembles fine breadcrumbs. Stir in sage. Add egg and milk and bind to a soft dough. Knead on a lightly floured surface and roll out to ½ in. thick. Using a cookie cutter, cut out 1½ in. rounds. Arrange scones on top of the casserole and brush with milk. Increase oven temperature to 400F. Return casserole to the oven and cook, uncovered, 15 to 20 minutes, until scones are risen and golden. Serve.

Makes 6 to 8 servings.

BRAISED LAMB & VEGETABLES

1 lb. firm, yellow-fleshed potatoes, cut into ¼ in.
   slices
2 cloves garlic, pounded to a paste
6 to 8 scallions, thinly sliced
2 medium-large artichoke bottoms, sliced
5 oz. chestnut mushrooms, chopped
handful parsley, finely chopped
1 tablespoon mixed fresh herbs, chopped
salt and freshly ground black pepper
3 tablespoons olive oil
4 lamb shoulder or loin chops
¾ cup full-bodied dry white wine

Preheat oven to 375F. In a bowl, combine potatoes, garlic, scallions, artichoke bottoms, mushrooms, parsley, mixed herbs, and seasoning. Place half the mixture in a heavy flameproof casserole. Heat oil in a skillet, add lamb, and brown on both sides. Drain on absorbent kitchen paper, then season and place in casserole.

Over the heat, stir wine into pan to dislodge cooking juices, bring to a boil, and pour over lamb. Cover with remaining vegetables and add sufficient water to come almost to the level of the vegetables. Bring to a boil, cover, and cook in the oven about 30 minutes. Uncover and cook an additional 1 hour. Add a little water if it seems to be drying out.

Makes 4 servings.

LAMB CHILINDRON

¼ cup olive oil
1½ lb. lean lamb, diced
salt and freshly ground black pepper
1 Spanish onion
2 cloves garlic, chopped
3 large red bell peppers, peeled, seeded, and cut into
   strips
4 beefsteak tomatoes, peeled (see page 12), seeded,
   and chopped
1 dried red chili, chopped
chopped fresh herbs, to garnish

Heat oil in a flameproof casserole. Season lamb and add to casserole.

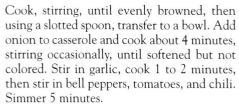

Cook, stirring, until evenly browned, then using a slotted spoon, transfer to a bowl. Add onion to casserole and cook about 4 minutes, stirring occasionally, until softened but not colored. Stir in garlic, cook 1 to 2 minutes, then stir in bell peppers, tomatoes, and chili. Simmer 5 minutes.

Return lamb, and any juices that have collected in bowl, to casserole. Cover tightly and cook gently about 1½ hours, until lamb is tender. Season if necessary. Serve garnished with chopped herbs.

Makes 6 servings.

LAMB WITH BLACK OLIVES

¼ cup olive oil
1½ lb. lean lamb, cut into small cubes
4 oz. side of pork, cut into small strips
2 cloves garlic, sliced
½ or 1 teaspoon chopped fresh oregano
¾ cup full-bodied white wine
1 fresh red chili, seeded and finely chopped
12 to 15 pitted black olives

Heat oil in a wide, shallow flameproof casserole. Add lamb, pork, and garlic and cook over a high heat to seal and brown meat.

In a small saucepan, boil oregano and wine 2 to 3 minutes. Stir into casserole, cover, and cook 30 minutes.

Stir chili and olives into casserole. Cover again and cook about 30 minutes until lamb is tender. If necessary, uncover casserole towards end of cooking time so liquid can evaporate to make a light sauce.

Makes 4 servings.

SPICED-COATED LAMB

4 cloves garlic
¼ teaspoon cumin seeds
1 tablespoon paprika
¼ teaspoon saffron threads, crushed
salt and freshly ground black pepper
1½ lb. lean boned lamb, cut into 1 to 1½ in. cubes
3 tablespoons olive oil
⅔ cup full-bodied dry white wine

Using a mortar and pestle, pound together garlic, cumin, paprika, saffron, salt, and pepper.

Put lamb into a bowl, add spice mixture and stir well but gently to coat lamb. Set aside 30 minutes.

Heat oil in a flameproof casserole, add lamb, and cook 5 to 7 minutes, stirring occasionally, until lamb has browned. Stir in wine and heat to simmering point. Cover tightly and cook gently about 30 to 40 minutes until meat is tender and sauce thickened.

Makes 4 servings.

LAMB IN GREEN SAUCE

2 tablespoons olive oil
1½ lb. boneless lamb, cut into pieces
1 Spanish onion, chopped
2 green bell peppers, seeded and chopped
3 cloves garlic, crushed
¾ cup dry white wine
⅔ cup water
1½ teaspoons chopped fresh thyme
salt and freshly ground black pepper
1 small round lettuce, sliced
2 tablespoons chopped fresh parsley
2 tablespoons chopped fresh mint
½ cup pine nuts
mint sprigs and pine nuts, to garnish

In a flameproof casserole, heat oil, add lamb, and fry, stirring occasionally, until evenly browned. Using a slotted spoon, remove lamb and set aside. Stir onion into casserole and cook about 4 minutes, stirring occasionally, until softened but not browned. Stir in bell peppers and garlic, cook 2 to 3 minutes, then stir in wine. Boil 1 minute.

Pour in water and bring to a boil. Lower heat so liquid is just simmering, then add lamb, thyme, and seasoning. Cover and cook gently about 1 hour. Stir in lettuce, parsley, mint, and pine nuts, cover, and cook an additional 10 to 15 minutes. Serve garnished with sprigs of mint and pine nuts.

Makes 4 servings.

LAMB WITH LEMON & GARLIC

3 tablespoons olive oil
2¼ lb. lean, boneless lamb, cut into 1 in. pieces
1 Spanish onion, finely chopped
3 cloves garlic, crushed
1 tablespoon paprika
3 tablespoons finely chopped fresh parsley
3 tablespoons lemon juice
salt and freshly ground black pepper
3 tablespoons dry white wine (optional)

Heat oil in a heavy flameproof casserole, add lamb, and cook, stirring occasionally, until lightly browned. Do this in batches if necessary so pieces are not crowded. Using a slotted spoon, transfer meat to a plate or bowl and reserve.

Stir onion into casserole and cook about 5 minutes, stirring occasionally, until softened. Stir in garlic, cook 2 minutes, then stir in paprika. When well blended, stir in lamb and any juices on plate or in bowl, parsley, lemon juice, and seasoning. Cover tightly and cook over very low heat 1¼ to 1½ hours, shaking casserole occasionally, until lamb is very tender. If necessary, add 3 tablespoons of wine or water.

Makes 4 to 6 servings.

POMEGRANATE LAMB

3 tablespoons vegetable oil
1 large onion, sliced
2 cloves garlic, finely chopped
1 in. piece fresh ginger, peeled and finely chopped
2¼ lb. lean lamb, diced
salt and freshly ground black pepper
juice 2 pomegranates, about 1¼ cups
1 teaspoon ground cumin
½ teaspoon ground cinnamon
¼ teaspoon ground nutmeg
3 cardamom pods, lightly crushed
⅓ cup plain yogurt
pomegranate seeds and chopped fresh mint, to garnish

Heat oil in a large flameproof casserole. Add onion, garlic, and ginger and cook 10 minutes until soft. Remove from the pan and set aside. In the same pan, brown lamb, in batches, and set aside. Return onion, garlic, ginger, and lamb to the pan. Season with salt and pepper. Gradually stir in pomegranate juice, allowing each addition to be absorbed before adding more. There should be very little liquid left.

Add cumin, cinnamon, nutmeg, and cardamom pods to the pan and stir 1 minute. Stir in yogurt. Cover the pan tightly and cook very gently, preferably on a heat diffuser, 30 to 40 minutes until lamb is tender. Check from time to time that the meat is not sticking and drying out too much. Add a little water if necessary. Garnish with pomegranate seeds and chopped mint and serve with rice.

Makes 4 to 6 servings.

LAMB STEAKS WITH PASTA

4 thick lamb leg steaks
salt and pepper
2 cloves garlic, sliced
14½ oz. can chopped tomatoes
⅓ cup olive oil
1 tablespoon chopped fresh marjoram
1 tablespoon chopped fresh parsley
1½ to 2 cups orzo (rice-shaped pasta)
salad leaves, to serve

Preheat oven to 400F. Season meat with salt and pepper. Place in a large baking pan.

Sprinkle meat with garlic. Add ⅔ cup water and tomatoes. Stir in olive oil, salt, pepper, marjoram, and parsley. Cook 40 minutes, basting from time to time and turning pieces of lamb over.

Add 1¼ cups boiling water and pasta. Stir in more salt and pepper. Cook an additional 40 minutes until pasta is cooked. If necessary, add more hot water. Serve with salad leaves.

Makes 4 servings.

CURRIED LAMB WITH ONIONS

1½ lb. shoulder of lamb, boned
1 teaspoon turmeric
1 teaspoon ground cumin
1 teaspoon ground coriander
1 in. piece fresh ginger, grated
2 cloves garlic, crushed
3 tablespoons vegetable oil
1 tablespoon sugar
4 large onions, sliced into thin rings
1 lb. potatoes, cut into large chunks
salt and cayenne pepper
1 teaspoon garam masala
rosemary sprigs, to garnish

Wipe lamb, trim and dice.

Put lamb in a non-metallic dish. Mix together turmeric, cumin, coriander, ginger, and garlic and add to lamb. Stir well, then cover loosely and leave in a cool place 2 to 3 hours. Heat oil in heavy-bottomed pan until smoking. Stir in sugar, then add onions and cook over a medium to high heat 10 minutes, stirring frequently, until a rich brown. Remove onions with a slotted spoon and set aside.

Add lamb to pan and fry until browned all over. Add potatoes and fry, stirring, 2 minutes. Return onions to pan, add 1 cup water, and season with salt and cayenne pepper. Bring to a boil and simmer, covered, 1¼ hours, or until lamb is tender, stirring occasionally. Stir in garam masala and serve, garnished with rosemary sprigs.

Makes 4 servings.

CURRIED LAMB WITH RAITA

3 tablespoons olive oil
2 onions, finely chopped
½ in. piece fresh ginger, peeled and grated
3 cloves garlic, crushed
1 teaspoon chili powder
1½ teaspoons turmeric
1½ teaspoons ground coriander
½ teaspoon each ground cumin and garam masala
1 lb. lamb fillet, diced
½ cup plain yogurt
salt and freshly ground black pepper
mint sprigs, to garnish
RAITA:
1¼ cups plain yogurt
1 small or ½ large cucumber, diced
1 tablespoon chopped fresh mint

Heat oil in a flameproof casserole. Add onions and cook, stirring occasionally, 5 minutes, until soft. Add ginger, garlic, chili powder, turmeric, coriander, cumin, and garam masala and cook, stirring, 2 minutes. Add lamb and cook, stirring, an additional 2 minutes, until browned.

Add yogurt, ½ cup water, and salt and pepper and stir well. Bring to a boil and simmer gently 45 minutes. Meanwhile, make raita. Mix together yogurt, cucumber, and chopped mint. Season with salt and pepper. Chill until required. Garnish lamb with mint sprigs and serve with raita.

Makes 4 servings.

LAMB & FLAGEOLET BEANS

4 x 8 oz. lamb shanks
4 cloves garlic, thinly sliced
2 tablespoons olive oil
1 onion, finely oil
1½ cups flageolet beans, soaked overnight
1¼ lb. tomatoes, peeled, seeded, and chopped
1 tablespoon tomato paste
⅔ cup red wine
bouquet garni
1 small bunch parsley, chopped
Italian parsley and bay leaves, to garnish

MEDITERRANEAN LAMB

1 eggplant, sliced
2 teaspoons salt
2 tablespoons olive oil, plus extra for brushing
1 lb. lamb fillet, diced
2 leeks, sliced
1 green bell pepper, chopped
14½ oz. can chopped tomatoes
1 clove garlic, crushed
2 zucchini, sliced
1 tablespoon tomato paste
1 tablespoon chopped fresh rosemary

Cut 4 incisions in each lamb shank. Insert a slice of garlic in each incision.

Place eggplant in a colander, sprinkle with salt, and let stand 30 minutes.

Heat oil in a heavy flameproof casserole, add lamb, and cook until browned all over. Remove and set aside. Add onion and remaining garlic to casserole and cook, stirring occasionally, 5 minutes, until soft but not browned.

Preheat oven to 375F. Heat oil in a flameproof dish. Add lamb and cook, stirring, 3 to 4 minutes, until browned all over. Add leeks and cook, stirring, 4 to 5 minutes, until soft. Stir in bell pepper, tomatoes, garlic, zucchini, tomato paste, and rosemary. Simmer 5 to 10 minutes.

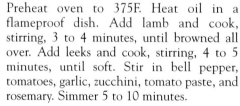

Drain and rinse beans and add to casserole with tomatoes, tomato paste, wine, bouquet garni, and salt and pepper. Return lamb to casserole, cover tightly, and cook gently 1 to 2 hours, until lamb and flageolet beans are tender. Discard bouquet garni and stir in parsley. Garnish and serve.

Makes 4 servings.

Rinse eggplant in cold water and pat dry with absorbent kitchen paper. Arrange eggplant slices on top of lamb mixture and brush with olive oil. Bake 30 to 40 minutes, until eggplant slices are golden brown and tender.

Makes 4 servings.

NAVARIN OF LAMB

1 tablespoon olive oil
2¼ lb. boneless lamb, diced
1 onion and 1 large carrot, finely chopped
pinch sugar
2 teaspoons all-purpose flour
½ cup dry white wine
2½ cups veal or chicken stock
bouquet garni
salt and freshly ground black pepper
3 ripe tomatoes, peeled, seeded, and chopped
3 small turnips, quartered
12 button onions
12 small new potatoes
12 baby carrots, halved or quartered
1 cup shelled fresh peas or small fava beans
parsley sprigs, to garnish

Heat oil in a heavy flameproof casserole, add lamb, and cook until browned all over. Remove with a slotted spoon and set aside. Add chopped onion and carrot and cook, stirring occasionally, 10 minutes, until browned. Sprinkle over sugar and flour and cook, stirring, until lightly browned. Add wine, stock, bouquet garni, and salt and pepper. Add tomatoes and bring to a boil, stirring. Return lamb to casserole, cover tightly, and cook gently 30 minutes.

Add turnips, onions, and potatoes, cover, and cook 20 minutes. Add carrots and cook 10 minutes. Add peas or beans and cook 5 to 7 minutes. Remove meat and vegetables with a slotted spoon, transfer to a warmed plate, and keep warm. Boil cooking juices to thicken slightly. Return lamb and vegetables to casserole and turn in sauce. Garnish with parsley and serve.

Makes 4 servings.

ROAST LEG OF LAMB WITH WINE

2¼ lb. lean leg of lamb
2 tablespoons olive oil
2 oz. salted anchovies, boned and rinsed
2 cloves garlic, chopped
1 tablespoon chopped fresh rosemary
8 juniper berries
2 tablespoons balsamic vinegar
salt and freshly ground bell pepper
⅔ cup dry white wine

Trim lamb of any excess fat. Heat oil in a flameproof casserole in which the lamb will fit snugly. Add lamb and brown all over. Remove and let cool.

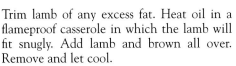

In a mortar, pound anchovies, garlic, rosemary, and 4 of the juniper berries to a paste. Stir in vinegar. Make small incisions all over lamb with a small sharp knife. Spread paste all over lamb, working it into the slits. Season. Replace lamb in casserole, and pour in wine. Crush remaining juniper berries and add to the casserole. Cover and simmer 1½ to 2 hours, until very tender, turning lamb every 20 minutes.

Carefully remove lamb from casserole and keep warm. Skim fat from sauce. Add a little water, if necessary, and bring to a boil, scraping the bottom of the pan to mix in the sediment. Serve sauce with lamb.

Makes 8 servings.

CARIBBEAN LAMB CURRY

MOROCCAN LAMB

1¾ lb. trimmed shoulder of lamb, cut into 1 in. cubes
finely grated zest and juice 1 lime
3 cloves garlic, crushed
3 tablespoons oil
1 large onion, chopped
2 teaspoons medium curry powder
1 teaspoon ground cumin
1 tablespoon hot pepper sauce
2 teaspoons molasses
2 tablespoons tomato paste
2 oz. creamed coconut
salt
1 tablespoon chopped cilantro

1 cup dried apricots
2 tablespoons olive oil
1 large onion, chopped
2¼ lb. boneless shoulder of lamb, diced
1 teaspoon ground cumin
½ teaspoon each ground coriander and cinnamon
salt and freshly ground black pepper
grated zest and juice ½ orange
1 teaspoon saffron threads
1 tablespoon ground almonds
1¼ cups lamb or chicken stock
1 tablespoon sesame seeds
Italian parsley sprigs, to garnish

Cut apricots in half and put in a bowl.

Place lamb in a bowl with lime zest and juice and garlic. Mix well, cover, and leave in a cool place 2 hours. In a flameproof casserole, heat oil. Add onion and cook 10 minutes until soft. Remove and set aside. Drain meat (reserve any marinade) and pat dry with absorbent kitchen paper. Add meat to hot oil, in batches, and fry until well browned. Return onions and browned meat to casserole.

Cover with ⅔ cup water and let soak overnight. Preheat the oven to 350F. Heat olive oil in a flameproof casserole. Add onion and cook gently 10 minutes until soft and golden. Add lamb, cumin, coriander, cinnamon, and salt and pepper and cook, stirring, 5 minutes.

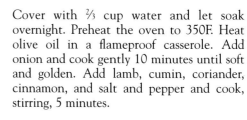

Stir in curry powder and cumin and cook an additional minute. Add hot pepper sauce, molasses, tomato paste, and creamed coconut and cook an additional 5 minutes. Add salt and about ⅔ cup water, to just cover meat. Bring to a boil, then reduce heat, cover, and simmer gently, stirring occasionally, 1½ to 2 hours until meat is tender. Stir in chopped cilantro. Serve with rice.

Makes 4 servings.

Add apricots and their soaking liquid. Stir in orange zest and juice, saffron, ground almonds, and enough stock to cover. Cover and cook in the oven 1 to 1½ hours until meat is tender, adding extra stock if necessary. Heat a skillet, add sesame seeds and dry-fry, shaking the pan, until golden. Sprinkle sesame seeds over meat, garnish with parsley, and serve.

Makes 4 to 6 servings.

MOROCCAN COUSCOUS

2¼ lb. trimmed lamb shoulder, cut into pieces
2 onions, chopped
⅓ cup chickpeas, soaked overnight
1 teaspoon ground ginger
pinch saffron threads
4 small turnips, cut into large pieces
4 small carrots, cut into large pieces
2½ cups regular couscous (not instant)
2 tablespoons smen or butter, melted
a little rosewater
⅓ cup raisins
4 medium zucchini, halved lengthwise
1 butternut squash, peeled and diced
2 tomatoes, quartered
2 tablespoons each chopped cilantro and parsley
harissa, to serve

Place lamb, onions, and chickpeas in the bottom of a couscoussière or large stockpot. Stir in ginger, saffron, and 1 teaspoon of pepper. Cover with water, bring to a boil, and simmer, covered, 45 minutes. Add turnips and carrots.

Place couscous grains in a large bowl. Dissolve 1 teaspoon salt in ⅔ cup water and sprinkle over couscous. Stir with your fingers, rubbing to separate grains and break up any lumps. When couscous has soaked up all the water, place in the top of a couscoussière, or in a colander lined with cheesecloth. Set the couscoussière or colander on top of the simmering stew.

If any steam escapes, wrap a strip of cloth around the top of the pan before placing couscous on top. Steam, covered, 20 minutes, occasionally drawing a fork through couscous grains to separate them. Turn couscous out on to a large wooden or earthenware dish. Sprinkle with a little soaked water, as before, and separate grains with your fingers.

Lightly rub in melted smen or butter and rosewater and put couscous back in the top part of the couscoussière or colander. Add raisins, zucchini, squash, tomatoes, salt, cilantro, and parsley to simmering stew then replace couscous over the pan. Steam an additional 30 minutes, occasionally fluffing couscous grains with a fork.

To serve, pile couscous on to a large wooden or earthenware serving dish. With a slotted spoon, transfer lamb and vegetables to the center of the dish. Pour over some of the broth. Stir some harissa into remaining broth and serve it separately.

Makes 6 servings.

Variation: The selection of vegetables can include beans, peas, and eggplant, but traditionally seven vegetables are used.

RED-COOKED LAMB FILLET

1 lb. lean lamb fillet
3 tablespoons dry sherry
½ in. piece fresh ginger, peeled and finely chopped
2 cloves garlic, thinly sliced
1 teaspoon five-spice powder
3 tablespoons dark soy sauce
1¼ cups vegetable stock
2 teaspoons sugar
2 teaspoons cornstarch mixed with 4 teaspoons water
salt and freshly ground bell pepper
shredded scallions, to garnish

Trim any excess fat and silver skin from lamb and discard. Cut lamb into ¾ in. cubes.

Cook lamb in a saucepan of boiling water 3 minutes. Drain well. Heat a nonstick or well-seasoned wok and add lamb, sherry, ginger, garlic, five-spice powder, and soy sauce. Bring to a boil, reduce heat, and simmer 2 minutes, stirring. Pour in stock, return to a boil, then simmer 25 minutes.

Add sugar, cornstarch mixture, salt, and pepper and stir until thickened. Simmer 5 minutes. Garnish with shredded scallions and serve on a bed of rice.

Makes 4 servings

MALAYSIAN LAMB CURRY

2 onions, chopped
3 cloves garlic, smashed
4 fresh red chilies, cored, seeded, and chopped
1 stalk lemon grass, chopped
1½ tablespoons chopped fresh ginger
2 teaspoons ground coriander
1 teaspoon ground cumin
3½ cups coconut milk
2¼ lb. lean mature lamb or mutton shoulder, cut into 2 in. cubes
juice 1 lime
1½ teaspoons light brown sugar
salt

Put onions, garlic, chilies, lemon grass, ginger, coriander, and cumin in a blender. Add about ⅔ cup of the coconut milk and mix together well. Pour into a large saucepan. Stir in 1¼ cups coconut milk and 3 cups water and bring to a simmer. Add lamb and lime juice. Simmer gently, uncovered, stirring occasionally, about 2 hours, until meat is tender and liquid has evaporated.

Add a little boiling water if liquid evaporates too quickly. Stir in remaining coconut milk and sugar. Add salt to taste and simmer about 5 minutes. Serve with boiled rice.

Makes 4 to 6 servings.

PORK

MARINATED SPICED PORK

3½ lb. leg of pork, skin and fat removed
1 tablespoon olive oil
4 oz. brown cap or shiitake mushrooms, sliced
thyme sprigs and celery leaves, to garnish
MARINADE:
2 tablespoons olive oil
1 onion, finely chopped
1 carrot, finely chopped
1 stalk celery, chopped
2 cups full-bodied red wine
6 juniper berries, crushed
8 peppercorns, crushed
¼ teaspoon ground allspice
bouquet garni
salt

To make marinade, heat oil in a heavy skillet, add onion and carrot, and cook, stirring occasionally, 5 minutes. Add celery and cook, stirring occasionally, until vegetables are browned. Add wine, juniper berries, peppercorns, allspice, bouquet garni, and salt. Let cool. Put pork in a non-metallic dish, pour over marinade, cover, and leave in a cool place 24 hours, turning pork occasionally. Preheat oven to 350F. Remove pork and vegetables with a slotted spoon and drain pork on absorbent kitchen paper. Strain marinade and set aside.

Heat oil in a heavy flameproof casserole just large enough to hold pork. Add pork and cook until browned all over. Remove and set aside. Add mushrooms and cook 5 minutes. Add reserved vegetables and put pork on top. Pour over marinade. Heat to almost simmering, cover, and cook in oven, turning occasionally, 2 to 2½ hours. Transfer to a warmed plate. Skim excess fat from sauce, then boil to thicken. Season. Carve pork, garnish, and serve with sauce.

Makes 4 to 6 servings.

PORK WITH PRUNES

1 cup large prunes
2½ cups dry white wine
3 tablespoons butter
4 pork chops
8 oz. mixed chopped onion, carrot and celery
1 cup veal or pork stock
bouquet garni
salt and freshly ground black pepper
squeeze of lemon juice

Put prunes in a bowl, pour over half the wine, and let soak overnight.

Heat 2 tablespoons butter in a heavy flameproof casserole, add chops, and cook quickly until browned on both sides. Remove and set aside. Add mixed chopped onion, carrot, and celery to casserole and cook, stirring occasionally, 5 to 7 minutes, until lightly browned. Stir in remaining wine and bring to a boil 2 to 3 minutes. Add stock and bring to a boil. Return chops to casserole, add bouquet garni and salt and pepper, cover tightly, and cook gently 45 minutes.

Add prunes and soaking liquid to casserole, bring to a boil, cover, and cook 30 minutes. Transfer pork and prunes to warmed serving plates and keep warm. Discard bouquet garni and boil sauce to thicken slightly. Reduce heat and gradually stir in remaining butter. Add lemon juice to taste, pour over pork and prunes, and serve.

Makes 4 servings.

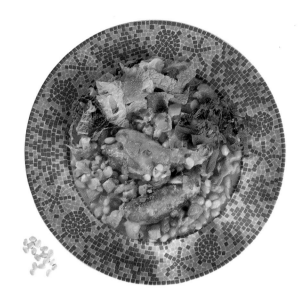

PORK WITH CIDER

2 tablespoons butter
4 pork chops
1 onion, finely chopped
2 teaspoons Calvados or brandy
1¼ cups dry cider
1 bay leaf
2 small cooking apples, peeled, cored and sliced
1 tablespoon lemon juice
2 tablespoons thick sour cream
salt and freshly ground black pepper
thyme sprigs and leaves, to garnish

Heat butter in a heavy flameproof casserole, add chops, and cook quickly until browned on both sides. Remove and set aside.

Preheat oven to 350F. Add onion to casserole and cook, stirring occasionally, 5 minutes, until soft. Add Calvados or brandy and set alight. When flames die down, stir in cider and bring to a boil. Return chops to casserole, add bay leaf and salt and pepper, cover tightly, and cook in oven 20 minutes.

Toss apples in lemon juice. Add to casserole, cover again, and cook 10 to 15 minutes. Remove pork and apples from casserole with a slotted spoon, transfer to warmed serving plates, and keep warm. Boil cooking liquid until lightly syrupy. Stir in thick sour cream, pour over pork and apples, garnish with thyme, and serve.

Makes 4 servings.

CASSOULET

1½ cups kidney beans, soaked overnight
2 tablespoons olive oil
6 oz. thick-cut smoked bacon, chopped
6 coarse-cut pork sausages
3 duck leg portions, halved
2 large onions, chopped
2 cloves garlic, crushed
12 oz. ripe tomatoes, peeled and chopped
1½ tablespoons tomato paste
½ cup dry white wine
large bunch fresh herbs
fresh herbs and chopped fresh parsley, to garnish

Drain and rinse beans. Put in a saucepan, cover with cold water, and bring to a boil.

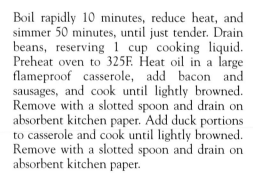

Boil rapidly 10 minutes, reduce heat, and simmer 50 minutes, until just tender. Drain beans, reserving 1 cup cooking liquid. Preheat oven to 325F. Heat oil in a large flameproof casserole, add bacon and sausages, and cook until lightly browned. Remove with a slotted spoon and drain on absorbent kitchen paper. Add duck portions to casserole and cook until lightly browned. Remove with a slotted spoon and drain on absorbent kitchen paper.

Add onions to casserole and cook, stirring occasionally, 7 minutes, until beginning to color. Return meats to casserole with beans, reserved cooking liquid, garlic, tomatoes, tomato paste, wine, and bunch of fresh herbs. Bring to a boil, cover, and cook in oven 1 to 1¼ hours, uncovering towards end of cooking to thicken juices. Garnish with sprigs of herbs and parsley and serve.

Makes 6 servings.

CARIBBEAN MEATBALLS

3 tablespoons oil
1 onion, finely chopped
1 lb. lean ground pork
1 cup fresh breadcrumbs
1 egg, beaten
¼ or ½ teaspoon chili powder
1 teaspoon ground coriander
salt and freshly ground black pepper
TOMATO SAUCE:
2 tablespoons oil
1 onion, finely chopped
1 clove garlic, crushed
3 stalks celery, chopped
14½ oz. can chopped tomatoes
1 teaspoon molasses
chopped cilantro, to garnish

In a saucepan, heat half the oil. Add onion and cook 10 minutes until soft. Set aside to cool. In a bowl, mix together onion, pork, breadcrumbs, egg, chili powder, ground coriander, and seasoning until thoroughly combined. Divide mixture into 24 and form into balls. Set aside.

To make sauce, heat oil in a saucepan. Add onion, garlic, and celery and cook 10 minutes until soft. Add tomatoes, molasses, and seasoning. Bring to a boil, cover, and simmer 15 minutes. Meanwhile, in a skillet, heat remaining oil. Fry meatballs, in batches if necessary, until brown on all sides. With a slotted spoon, transfer meatballs to sauce. Simmer gently 20 minutes. Serve garnished with chopped cilantro.

Makes 4 to 6 servings.

PORK WITH TAMARIND

4 dried red chilies, cored and seeded
1 large onion, chopped
4 candlenuts or cashews
2 tablespoons vegetable oil
1½ lb. pork shoulder, cut into large bite-size pieces
2 tablespoons tamarind paste
2 tablespoons dark soy sauce
1 tablespoon yellow bean sauce
1 tablespoon light brown sugar
sliced fresh chilies, to garnish (optional)

Put chilies in a blender. Add ¼ cup hot water and leave until slightly softened. Add onion and nuts; mix to a smooth paste.

In a sauté pan, preferably nonstick, heat oil over medium-high heat. Add meat in batches and fry until an even light brown. Using a slotted spoon, transfer to absorbent kitchen paper to drain.

Add chili paste to pan and fry about 5 minutes. Stir in pork, tamarind paste, soy sauce, yellow bean sauce, sugar, and 1½ cups water. Bring to a simmer, cover pan, then cook gently 30 to 40 minutes, stirring occasionally, until pork is very tender. Serve garnished with sliced fresh chilies, if desired.

Makes 4 servings.

DRY PORK CURRY

12 oz. lean boneless pork, trimmed and cut into
¾ in. cubes
1 tablespoon light brown sugar
12 oz. potatoes
2 carrots
8 oz. shallots
1 tablespoon sunflower oil
1 in. piece fresh ginger, peeled and finely chopped
2 tablespoons Madras curry paste
⅔ cup coconut milk
1¼ cups chicken stock
salt and freshly ground bell pepper
2 tablespoons chopped cilantro

In a bowl, mix together pork and brown sugar and set aside. Cut potatoes and carrots into ¾ in. chunks. Peel and halve shallots.

Heat oil in a nonstick or well-seasoned wok and stir-fry pork, ginger, potatoes, carrots, and shallots 2 to 3 minutes or until lightly browned. Blend curry paste with coconut milk, stock, salt, and pepper. Stir into pork mixture and bring to the boil. Reduce heat and simmer 40 minutes. Sprinkle with cilantro, and serve on a bed of rice.

Makes 4 servings.

PORK IN CIDER & ORANGE

3 tablespoons olive oil
flour for coating
salt and freshly ground black pepper
1½ lb. boned and rolled loin of pork
1 small Spanish onion, sliced
1¼ cups well-flavored dry cider
juice 1 large juicy orange
peel from ¼ orange, cut into fine strips
pinch ground cinnamon
pinch sugar (optional)
thin orange slices, parsley sprigs, and slivered toasted almonds, to garnish

Heat oil in a heavy flameproof casserole. Put flour on a plate and season with salt and pepper. Roll pork in seasoned flour to coat evenly and lightly. Add to casserole and brown evenly about 10 minutes. Remove and keep warm. Stir onion into casserole and cook over a low heat about 20 minutes, stirring occasionally, until very soft and lightly browned. Stir in cider, orange juice and strips of peel, and cinnamon. Bring to a boil and simmer 2 to 3 minutes.

Return pork to casserole, turn it in sauce, cover, and cook gently about 45 minutes until pork is tender. Transfer pork to a serving dish and boil sauce, if necessary, to thicken lightly. Adjust seasoning and level of cinnamon, and add a pinch of sugar, if desired. Pour sauce over pork and garnish with orange slices, parsley sprigs, and toasted slivered almonds.

Makes 4 servings.

CARAWAY POT ROAST

1 tablespoon olive oil
2½ lb. arm shoulder of pork, boned
2 large onions, chopped
4 medium parsnips, cut into chunks
¼ cup caraway seeds
½ teaspoon freshly grated nutmeg
salt and freshly ground black pepper
1 cup chicken stock
1 cup red wine
thyme sprigs, to garnish

Preheat oven to 350F. Heat oil in a large flameproof casserole. Add pork and cook until browned all over.

Remove meat from the casserole. Add onions and parsnips and cook, stirring occasionally, 7 minutes, until golden. Lay pork on top of vegetables. Mix together caraway seeds and nutmeg and sprinkle on top of pork. Season with salt and pepper. Pour stock and wine around pork. Cover tightly and cook in the oven 2 hours, or until pork is cooked through and tender. Remove pork from the casserole and keep warm.

Remove vegetables from the casserole with a slotted spoon. Bring sauce to a boil and boil until reduced and thickened. Season with salt and pepper. Slice meat, garnish with thyme sprigs, and serve with vegetables and sauce.

Makes 6 to 8 servings.

Note: Skim any fat from the surface of the sauce before serving, if you prefer.

HARVEST CASSEROLE

2 tablespoons olive oil
4 sparerib pork chops
1 large onion, sliced
2 leeks, chopped
1 clove garlic, crushed
2 medium parsnips, cut into chunks
2 carrots, cut into chunks
1 teaspoon dried sage
2 tablespoons all-purpose flour
1¼ cups beef stock
1¼ cups apple juice
salt and freshly ground black pepper
2 small eating apples
1½ cups self-rising flour
⅔ cup shredded suet
1 teaspoon mixed dried herbs

Preheat oven to 325F. Heat the oil in a large flameproof casserole. Add chops and cook 2 to 3 minutes on each side until browned. Remove from the casserole and drain on absorbent kitchen paper. Add onion, leeks, and garlic and cook, stirring occasionally, 5 minutes, until soft. Add parsnips, carrots, and sage and cook 2 minutes. Add all-purpose flour and cook, stirring, 1 minute. Gradually stir in stock and apple juice. Season with salt and pepper and bring to a boil.

Replace chops, cover, and cook in the oven 1¼ hours, or until pork is tender. Meanwhile, core and roughly chop apples and set aside. Mix together self-rising flour, suet, dried herbs, and salt and pepper. Add ¾ cup water and bind to a firm dough. Divide dough into eight small dumplings. Stir apples into the casserole. Place dumplings on top, return to the oven, and cook, uncovered, 20 minutes. Serve.

Makes 4 servings.

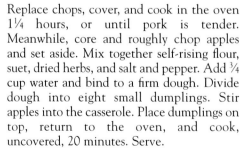

PORK WITH APPLE BALLS

2 tablespoons olive oil
6 oz. boneless pork loin chops
3 medium onions, sliced
2 cloves garlic, crushed
12 plum tomatoes, peeled (see page 12) and chopped
⅔ cup beef stock
¼ cup red wine vinegar
5 crisp eating apples
2 tablespoons lemon juice
salt and freshly ground black pepper

Preheat oven to 350F. Heat olive oil in an ovenproof casserole. Add chops and cook 3 minutes on each side, until browned.

Remove chops and keep warm. Add onions to the casserole and cook, stirring occasionally, 5 minutes, until soft. Add garlic and tomatoes. Return chops to the casserole and pour in stock and red wine vinegar. Bring to a boil. Meanwhile, peel apples and use a melon baller to cut out ball-shaped pieces. Put balls into a bowl of water with lemon juice, to prevent apple discoloring. Chop remaining apple and add to the casserole. Cover and cook in the oven 1 hour.

Remove chops from the casserole and keep warm. Pour sauce into a blender or food processor and process 1 minute. Season with salt and pepper. Return to the pan with chops and apple balls. Cook gently 15 minutes, until apple balls are just tender.

Makes 4 servings.

FRAGRANT HAM

3 lb. piece ham
2 medium parsnips, halved lengthwise
5 carrots, cut into chunks
1 lb. rutabaga, cut into chunks
2 stalks celery, cut into chunks
1 tablespoon brown sugar
1 tablespoon red wine vinegar
1 tablespoon black peppercorns
6 cloves
oregano sprigs, to garnish

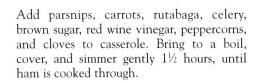

Put ham in a flameproof casserole. Cover with cold water and let soak 1 hour. Drain and cover with fresh water.

Add parsnips, carrots, rutabaga, celery, brown sugar, red wine vinegar, peppercorns, and cloves to casserole. Bring to a boil, cover, and simmer gently 1½ hours, until ham is cooked through.

Lift out ham, slice, and arrange on warmed serving plates. Remove vegetables with a slotted spoon, arrange around ham, garnish with oregano sprigs, and serve.

Makes 6 to 8 servings.

SPICY SPARERIBS

2¼ lb. spareribs
1 large onion, finely chopped
3 cloves garlic, crushed
2 bay leaves
1 teaspoon ground cumin
1 teaspoon mild chili powder
3 tablespoons cider vinegar
2 tablespoons tomato ketchup
1 tablespoon soy sauce
2 tablespoons clear honey
14½ oz. can chopped tomatoes

Preheat oven to 400F. Put spareribs in a flameproof casserole and cook in the oven 30 minutes.

Remove ribs with a slotted spoon and set aside. In a bowl, mix together onion, garlic, bay leaves, cumin, chili powder, cider vinegar, tomato ketchup, soy sauce, honey, and tomatoes. Season with salt and pepper.

Stir tomato mixture into the casserole. Bring to a boil and simmer 5 minutes. Add ribs, turn to coat with sauce, and cover. Return to the oven and cook an additional 30 minutes.

Makes 4 servings.

PORK WITH PEARS

2 tablespoons olive oil
2 onions, chopped
2¼ lb. boned lean pork, diced
1 cup red wine
grated zest ½ orange
½ cinnamon stick
salt and pepper
2 pears
2 teaspoons clear honey
chopped cilantro leaves, strips of orange peel and pita bread, to garnish

In a flameproof casserole, heat oil. Add onions; cook until soft. Push to side of pan, turn up heat, and brown meat in batches.

Add wine, orange zest, cinnamon stick, salt, pepper, and 1¼ cups water. Bring to simmering point, then cover casserole and cook 1 hour.

Peel, core, and slice pears and place on top of meat. Drizzle honey over pears. Cover pan and simmer gently 30 to 40 minutes until meat is tender. Garnish with chopped cilantro leaves, strips of orange peel, and pieces of pita bread.

Makes 6 servings.

Note: This recipe is traditionally made with quinces. If quinces are available, use them instead of pears.

PORK IN SPINACH SAUCE

1½ lb. fresh spinach, well rinsed
salt
1½ lb. lean boneless pork
3 tablespoons vegetable oil
2 onions, finely sliced
4 cloves garlic, crushed
1 in. piece fresh ginger, grated
3 tablespoons garam masala
½ teaspoon turmeric
1 bay leaf
2 tomatoes, peeled (see page 12) and chopped
2 fresh green chilies, seeded and chopped
⅔ cup plain yogurt
tomato slices and bay leaves, to garnish

Trim stems from spinach and cook leaves in boiling salted water 2 to 3 minutes, until tender. Drain thoroughly and rinse under cold running water. Put in a blender or food processor fitted with a metal blade and process to a smooth purée. Set aside. Preheat oven to 325F. Cut pork into 1 in. cubes. Heat oil in a large skillet and fry pork until browned all over. Transfer to a casserole using a slotted spoon.

Add onions to pan and cook, stirring, 10 to 15 minutes, until a rich brown. Add garlic, ginger, garam masala, turmeric, bay leaf, tomatoes, and chilies. Cook, stirring, 2 to 3 minutes, until tomatoes have softened. Add yogurt and ⅔ cup water and stir. Pour over pork, cover, and cook 1¼ to 1½ hours, until pork is cooked through. Remove bay leaf, stir in spinach and salt, re-cover, and cook an additional 10 minutes. Garnish and serve.

Makes 4 servings.

INDONESIAN-STYLE PORK

1 tablespoon seasoned flour
1¼ lb. pork fillet, cut into small cubes
2 or 3 tablespoons vegetable oil
1 onion, cut lengthwise in half and thinly sliced
2 cloves garlic, finely chopped
1 in. piece fresh ginger, peeled and cut into matchstick strips
½ teaspoon sambal oelek (see Note) or Chinese chili sauce
¼ cup Indonesian soy sauce or dark soy sauce sweetened with 1 tablespoon sugar
cilantro leaves, to garnish

In a medium bowl, combine seasoned flour and pork cubes and toss to coat well.

Heat the wok until very hot. Add 2 tablespoons of the oil and swirl to coat wok. Shake pork cubes to remove any excess flour, then add to wok and stir-fry 3 to 4 minutes until browned on all sides, adding a little more oil if necessary. Push pork to one side, add onion, garlic, and ginger, and stir-fry 1 minute, tossing all ingredients.

Add sambal oelek or chili sauce, soy sauce, and ⅔ cup water; stir. Bring to a boil, reduce heat to low, and simmer gently, covered, 20 to 25 minutes, stirring occasionally, until pork is tender and sauce thickened. Garnish with cilantro and serve with fried rice or noodles.

Makes 4 servings.

Note: Sambal oelek is a very hot, chili-based Indonesian condiment available in specialist or oriental food stores.

LENTIL & CHORIZO POTAJE

CHORIZO & CHICKPEA POTAJE

2½ cups green or brown lentils
1 Spanish onion, chopped
2 carrots, chopped
6 cloves garlic
6 to 8 oz. cooking chorizo
4 oz. piece side of pork, rind removed
1 bay leaf
2 beefsteak tomatoes, peeled (see page 12), seeded,
   and chopped
1 red bell pepper, seeded and chopped
1½ tablespoons olive oil
1 Spanish onion, finely chopped
salt and freshly ground black pepper

1⅓ cups chickpeas, soaked overnight, then drained
¼ cup olive oil
1 slice bread, crusts removed
1 Spanish onion, finely chopped
8 oz. cooking chorizo, thickly sliced
3 beefsteak tomatoes, peeled (see page 12), seeded,
   and chopped
1 tablespoon paprika
¼ or ½ teaspoon cumin seeds, finely crushed
1 lb. spinach, trimmed and chopped
3 cloves garlic

Cook chickpeas in 1½ times their volume of
boiling water 1½ to 2 hours until tender.

Put lentils, chopped onion, carrots, garlic,
chorizo, pork, bay leaf, tomatoes, and bell
pepper into a flameproof casserole or a
saucepan. Just cover with water and bring to
boil. Cover and simmer gently about 30
minutes, until lentils are tender, pork is
cooked, and there is sufficient liquid left to
make a thick soup.

Meanwhile, heat 2 tablespoons oil in a small
skillet, add bread, and fry until golden on
both sides. Remove and drain on absorbent
kitchen paper. Add onion to pan and cook
slowly, stirring occasionally, 5 minutes. Add
chorizo and cook further 5 to 10 minutes
until onion has softened but not colored.
Stir tomatoes into onion and cook, stirring
occasionally, about 10 minutes.

Meanwhile, heat oil in a heavy-bottomed
casserole, add finely chopped onion, and
cook very gently about 15 minutes, stirring
occasionally, until soft and lightly
caramelized. Stir into lentils and season with
salt and pepper. Discard bay leaf. Slice
chorizo and pork and return to lentils and
heat through.

Makes 4 to 5 servings.

Heat remaining oil in a saucepan, stir in
paprika and cumin, then add spinach. Cook
until spinach has wilted. Using a mortar and
pestle, pound garlic with a pinch of salt. Add
fried bread and pound again. Drain
chickpeas, reserving liquid. Stir chickpeas
into spinach with tomato and garlic mixtures
and ¾ cup chickpea liquid. Cover pan and
simmer about 30 minutes; add more liquid if
mixture becomes too dry.

Makes 4 servings.

INDEX

INDEX